Lyman Horace Weeks

Origin and Development of the Automobile

Lyman Horace Weeks

Origin and Development of the Automobile

ISBN/EAN: 9783845713083

Erscheinungsjahr: 2011

Erscheinungsort: Bremen, Deutschland

www.unikum-verlag.de | office@unikum-verlag.de

Bei diesem Titel handelt es sich um den Nachdruck eines historischen, lange vergriffenen Buches. Da elektronische Druckvorlagen für diese Titel nicht existieren, musste auf alte Vorlagen zurückgegriffen werden. Hieraus zwangsläufig resultierende Qualitätsverluste bitten wir zu entschuldigen.

AN ACCOUNT OF THE LIVES AND THE WORK OF THOSE WHO HAVE BEEN IDENTIFIED WITH THE INVENTION AND DEVELOPMENT OF SELF-PROPELLED VEHICLES ON THE COMMON ROADS

FOREWORD

FOREWORD

IN a large sense the history of the rise of the automobile has been a history of some of the foremost inventors, mechanical engineers, manufacturers and active business men of more than a full century. The subject of self-propelled vehicles on the common roads has enlisted the faculties of many men whose minds have been engrossed with the study and the solution of mechanical and engineering problems, purely from an absorbing love of science; it has had the financial support of those whose energies are constantly and forcefully exerted in the industrial and commercial activities of the age; it has received the merited consideration of those who regard as of paramount importance any addition to the sum of successful human endeavor and any influence that contributes to the further advance of modern civilization.

Along these lines of thought this book of AUTOMOBILE BIOGRAPHIES has been prepared. On its pages are sketches of the lives and the work of those who have been most active in planning, inventing and perfecting the modern horseless highway vehicle, in adapting it to the public needs for pleasure or business and in promoting its usefulness and broadening the field of its utility.

Included herein are accounts of the pioneer inventors, the noted investigators and the contemporaneous workers who have helped to make the automobile in its many forms the most remarkable mechanical success of to-day and the most valuable and epoch-making addition to the conveniences of modern social, industrial and commercial life. These sketches have been carefully prepared from the best sources of information, works of reference, personal papers and so on, and are believed to be thoroughly accurate and reliable. Much of the information contained in them has been derived from exceedingly rare old volumes and papers that are not generally accessible, and it comes with a full flavor of newness. Much also has been acquired from original sources and has never before been given to the public.

The investigator into this subject will find, doubtless, to his very great surprise, that the story of the pioneer inventors, who, in the early part of the nineteenth century, experimented with the problems of the steam road carriage, has been recorded voluminously and with much detail. It was a notable movement, that absorbed the abundant attention of inventors, manufacturers and the public at large at that time.

Writers of that day recorded with a great deal of particularity the experimenting with boilers, engines, machinery and carriages, and the promoting of companies for the transportation of passengers and the hauling of goods. Modern students and historians of this subject find themselves greatly indebted to the writers of that epoch, like Gordon, Herbert and others, who preserved, with such painstaking care, for future generations, as well as for their own time, the account of the lives and labors of such men as Watt, Trevithick, Maceroni, Hancock and others. Every modern work upon this subject draws generously from those sources.

Concerning the later period from the middle of the century that has just ended, down to the present time, there is less concrete information, readily available. With the cessation of public interest in the matter and its general relegation into the background, by inventors, engineers and those who had previously been financial backers of the experimenting, writers ceased to give the subject the enthusiastic attention that they had before bestowed upon it. Records of that period are scant, partly because there was so little to record and partly because no one cared to record even that little.

Until comparatively recent times the historian of the self-propelled vehicle, who was so much in evidence seventy-five years ago, had not reappeared. Even now his work is generally of a desultory character, voluminous, but largely ephemeral. It is widely scattered, not easily accessible and already considerably forgotten from day to day. Especially of the men of the last half century, who have made the present-day automobile possible and are now contributing to its greater future, the following pages present much that has never been brought together in this form. It is both history and the material for history.

It is believed that these sketches will be found peculiarly interesting and permanently valuable. Individually they are clear presentations of the achievements of some of the most distinguished engineers and inventors of the last hundred years. Collectively they present a complete story of the inception and gradual development of the automobile from the first clumsy steam wagons of Cugnot, Trevithick, Evans and others to the perfected carriage of to-day.

The chapter on The Origin and Development of the Automobile is a careful study and review of the conditions that attended the attempts to install the first common road steam carriages, the tentative experimenting with bicycles, tricycles and other vehicles in the middle of the last century and the renaissance of the last two decades. Several of the illustrations are from old and rare prints, and others are from photographs.

It is not possible to set down here all the authorities that have been consulted in the preparation of this work. Special acknowledgment, however, must be made to The Engineering Magazine for permission to use text and photographs, and to J. G. Pangborn for permission to use a great deal of interesting information regarding the early steam inventors contained in his work, The World's Railway, and to reproduce portrait sketches of Trevithick, Murdoch, and Read, from the same valuable volume.

LYMAN HORACE WEEKS.

NEW YORK, January, 1905.

ORIGIN AND DEVELOPMENT OF THE AUTOMOBILE

ORIGIN AND DEVELOPMENT OF THE AUTOMOBILE

STRANGE EARLY VEHICLES

He who would fully acquaint himself with the history of the inception and growth of the idea of travel by self-propelled vehicles on the public highways must go further back in the annals of the past than he is likely first to anticipate. Nearly three centuries ago men of mechanical and scientific turns of mind were giving attention to the subject, although their thoughts at that time were mostly confined to the realms of imaginative speculation. Even before that philosophers occasionally dreamed of what might be in some far off time. Roger Bacon, in the thirteenth century, looking into the distant future, made this prediction: "It will be possible to construct chariots so that without animals they may be moved with incalculable speed." It was several hundred years before men were ready to give practical attention to this idea, and about 1740 good Bishop Berkeley could only make this as a prediction and not a realization: "Mark me, ere long we shall see a pan of coals brought to use in place of a feed of oats."

But the ancients, in a way, anticipated even Roger Bacon and Bishop Berkeley, for Heliodorus refers to a triumphal chariot at Athens that was moved by slaves who worked the machinery, and Pancirollus also alludes to such chariots.

Horseless Wagons in China

Approaching the seventeenth century the investigator finds that definite examples are becoming more numerous, even if as yet not very practical. China, which, like Egypt, seems to have known and buried many ideas centuries before the rest of the world achieved them, had horseless vehicles before 1600. These merit, at least, passing attention even though they were not propelled by an engine, for the present automobile is the outgrowth of that old idea to eliminate the horse as the means of travel.

Matthieu Ricci, 1552-1610, a Jesuit missionary in China, told how in that country a wagon not drawn by horses or other animals was in common use. In an early collection of travels this vehicle was described as follows: "This river is so cloyed with ships because it is not frozen in winter that the way is stopped with multitude; which made Ricius exchange his way by water into another (more strange to us) by waggon, if we may so call it, which had but one wheel, so built that one might sit in the middle as 'twere on horseback, and on each side another, the waggoner putting 't swiftly and safely forwards with levers or barres of wood (those waggons driven by wind and gayle he mentions not.)" It was somewhat later than this that China was indebted to that other famous Jesuit missionary, Verbiest, for his steam carriage, which, however, was not much more than a toy.

Manually Propelled Vehicles

But in the seventeenth century most attention seems to have been given to devising carriages that should be moved by the hand or foot power of man. The auto car that was run in the streets of Nuremberg, Germany, by Johann Hautsch, in 1649, was of this description, and that of Elie Richard, the physician, of La Rochelle, France, about the same time, was of the same class.

Not long after this Potter, of England, came along in 1663 with a mechanical cart designed to travel on legs, and in the same year the celebrated Hooke presented to the Royal Society of England a plan for some sort of a machine by which one could "walk upon the land or water with swiftness, after the manner of a crane." It does not quite appear what that cart and that machine were. One authority thinks that the Hooke patent was for a one-wheel vehicle supposed to be propelled by a person inside the wheel. Then, also, there was Beza, another French physician, with a mechanical vehicle in 1710.

Other French and English Experiments

In fact, the interest in carriages worked by man power extended from the seventeenth well into the nineteenth century. Soon after the time of Beza, mechanical chariots, modeled after the Richard coach, were advertised to be run in London, but it does not appear that they met with public favor. Scientists and others gave much thought to the subject, both in England and in France. John Vevers, master of the boarding-school at Ryegate, Surrey, came out with a carriage that was evidently copied from that of Richard. Other forms of carriages worked by hand or foot power of man were described in the periodicals of the time. George Black, of

Berwick-on-the-Tweed, built a wagon to be run by hand power in 1768. In England, John Ladd, of Trowbridge, Wilts, in 1757; John Beaumont, of Ayrshire, in 1788, and in France, Thomas in 1703, Gerard in 1711, Ferry in 1770, and Maillard, Blanchard and Meurice, in 1779, and others, were most active during this period.

It was well into the nineteenth century before this idea was wholly abandoned. Edmund Cartwright, inventor of the hand loom, contributed to the experimenting, and the 1831 patent to Sir James C. Anderson was for a very imposing vehicle rowed by twenty-four men.

Compressed Air Power

At the same time that the steam engineers in England were bringing out their vehicles, 1800-35, others were at work on the problem of compressed air carriages. Among these was W. Mann, of Brixton, who, in 1830, published in London a pamphlet, entitled A Description of a New Method of Propelling Locomotive Machines, and of Communicating Power and Motion to All Other Kinds of Machinery, and it contained a lithograph of the proposed carriage. Sir George Medhurst, of England, about 1800, with his proposed regular line of coaches run by compressed air was, perhaps, the most conspicuous experimenter into this method of propulsion.

Sailing Carriages on Land

Many men long speculated upon the possibility of wind propulsion on land as well as upon the sea. The most ambitious attempt in that line was the sailing chariot of Simon Stevin, of The Hague, in 1600. Vehicles of this kind were built by others, and in 1695 Sir Humphrey Mackworth applied sails to wagons on the tramways at his colliery at Neath, South Wales. The Frenchman, Du Quet, in 1714, and the Swiss clergyman, Genevois, proposed to get power from windmills mounted on their wagons. More curious even than these was the carriage drawn by kites, the invention of George Pocock, in 1826.

The Steam Carriage Predicted

But all these and other fantastic devices never got beyond the experimental stage, and nothing of a substantial, practical character was ever evolved from them. It remained for the latter part of the eighteenth century to see the subject taken up seriously and considered in a way that promised definite results. And it was steam that then brought the matter strongly to the front.

It is true that Sir Isaac Newton tentatively suggested the possibility of carriage propulsion by steam about 1680, but his suggestion lay dormant for nearly a century. Then the growing knowledge of the power of steam and the possibilities in the new element turned men's thoughts again very forcibly to this theme. The stationary engine had shown its usefulness, and the consideration of making this stationary machine movable, and therefore available for transportation, naturally followed.

Dr. Erasmus Darwin is said to have urged James Watt and Matthew Boulton to build a fiery chariot as early as 1765. In his poem, The Botanic Garden, famous in that day, Dr. Darwin, like a prophet crying in the wilderness, sang of the future of steam in these lines:

"Soon shall thy arm, unconquered steam, afar
Drag the slow barge, or drive the rapid car;
On, on wide waving wings, expanded bear
The flying chariot through the field of air;
Fair crews triumphant, leaning from above,
Shall wave their fluttering 'kerchiefs as they move,
Or warrior bands alarm the gaping crowds,
And armies shrink beneath the shadowy clouds."

These lines may indeed be fairly interpreted as anticipating in prophetic prediction the modern motor airship, as well as the motor car.

The First Steam Vehicles

It was considerably later than this that the dream of Dr. Darwin approached to realization at the hands of the steam engine inventors and builders. Aside from Nicholas Joseph Cugnot, the French army officer who, about 1769, constructed an artillery wagon propelled by a high-pressure engine, those who first built successful self-propelled vehicles for highway travel were the famous engineers of England and Scotland, who harnessed steam and developed the high-pressure engine in the last half of the eighteenth century and the first half of the nineteenth. James Watt patented, in 1782, a double-acting engine, which he planned might be "applied to give motion to wheel carriages," the engine to be portable; but he never put the patent to trial. He was followed by George Stephenson, Richard Trevithick, Walter Hancock, Goldsworthy Gurney, David Gordon, William Brunton and others in England, and Oliver

Evans, Nathan Read and Thomas Blanchard in the United States, with two score or more contemporaries. For more than half a century steam vehicles of various types were invented by these engineers and many of them were brought into practical use.

Soon after the end of the first quarter of the nineteenth century the interest in steam carriages had assumed large proportions in England. In 1833 there were no less than twenty such vehicles, either completed or in hand, around London, and a dozen corporations had been organized to build and run them over stated routes.

Alexander Gordon, the eminent engineer, wrote a book, entitled Treatise Upon Elemental Locomotion, that went into three editions inside of four years. He also brought out two special journals covering this field of mechanics. The Mechanic's Magazine, and other publications, also gave much attention to the subject, and the steam-carriage literature of the period became very voluminous.

Popular Prejudice Aroused

For a time it looked as though the new vehicle was destined to a permanency and to accomplish a revolution in the methods of travel on the high-roads. But several things arose to determine otherwise. There sprang up an unreasoning senseless hostility to any substitute for the horse as the agent of vehicular traffic. The stage-coach drivers were afraid that they would be thrown out of work. Breeders of horses foresaw the destruction of their business, when horses should no longer be in demand. Farmers were sure that with horses superseded by steam, they would never be able to sell any more oats. This public animosity manifested itself wherever the steam carriages went. The coaches were hooted at and stoned amid cries of "down with machinery." Stones and other obstacles were placed in the roads, trenches were dug to trap the unsuspicious driver and stretches of roadway were dug up and made into quagmires to stall the machines. Parliament was called upon and enacted excessive highway tolls, especially directed at steam carriages. Another law that stood on the statute books of Great Britain until within comparatively recent times compelled every self-propelled vehicle moving on the highway to be preceded by a man walking and carrying a red flag.

The Beginning of Railroads

All this was undoubtedly due, in a large measure, if not wholly, to what was then known as the Turn Pike Trusts, which, in conjunction with the stage-line companies, in many cases, were owners of a thousand and more horses. The latter, quite naturally, objected to the introduction of the mechanical vehicle, while the former had such relations to them that both their interests were identical.

But above all things, the great art of railroading had already grown from infant existence to a condition of great possibilities, which were now to be finally determined by a success, not alone mechanical and in the eyes of the inventor, but measured by the balance sheets of the companies of individuals who had made possible the construction of the various experimental locomotives or experimental lines then being operated in England and elsewhere. Just at this time, in the thirties of the nineteenth century, seems to have been the crucial point. The arguments of the engineers on the question of sufficient traction of the iron-shod wheels on iron or other hard railways, while given due consideration, were not wholly convincing, at least to the people investing their money in the enterprises; the profits were to tell in the final conclusion, and it would seem that the great era of railroading might be considered to have had its actual birth at this time, because:

The first dividend was paid on one of the great railroad enterprises.

Influence of the First Dividend

For the time being that seemed to sound the death knell of the common road steam-propelled vehicle. The engineers so strongly advocating the railroad had proven their various propositions in the eyes of those who had the financial powers to engage in the extensive introduction and development of the new means of transportation. Further demonstration, extensively exploited, was also made to the satisfaction of those investors, that vehicles could be pulled with less power on a hard roadbed such as a railway, than on an uneven and sometimes soft path such as common roads. It seems clear that these and various other arguments, heartily urged at that time, and, in some cases, unquestionable from a technical standpoint, were really decided by that first dividend. And the common road vehicle with the support and enthusiasm of its backers largely withdrawn from it dropped to a position greatly subordinate to the other branch of transportation.

The Steam Road Vehicle Again

On the other hand, the development which came in the next few decades in the railroad department brought also a renewed demand for common road vehicles for certain classes of work or for certain localities. The steam vehicle for stationary purposes, and also for the locomotive, were being rapidly developed and refined. The railroad settled down to the idea of a power unit drawing numerous wagons. That has been consistently adhered to to the present day, and only in the past decade have we gone back to the old and first principles of embodying the mechanical propelling means in the same vehicle that transports the passengers or goods. So, while Hancock and his worthy contemporaries passed into history, other common road steam advocates continued their isolated attempts up to and past the middle of the nineteenth century, although without any such general enthusiasm as prevailed in the twenties and early thirties.

New Generation of Inventors

Many attempts in America, such as those of Fisher, Dudgeon, and others, and the work in England by numerous inventors and machine manufacturers, such as Tangye, Hilditch, Snowden, F. Hill, Jr., aided by the engineers, Macadam, Telford and M'Neil, who were improving the common roads so that they might approach the advantageous conditions of the railroad, assume prominence in connection with that period of the history. Rickett's carriage, in 1858; Carrett's, in 1862; Boulton's, in 1867; Catley's, in 1869, and others, were among the finger-posts of that time, pointing to more notable achievements of the future.

But in England the Act of Parliament, passed in 1836 and in force almost to to-day, known as the Locomotive Act, was the deterrent to progress in common road steam locomotion. This condition even continued after the select committee of Parliament, in 1873, endeavored to remove some of the restrictions, but succeeded only in producing the Act of 1878, which in no way improved the position of the common road vehicle.

In France and on the Continent political conditions doubtless mitigated against any general advance, and though this period included the great development of machinery and construction which paved the way for the future, it is not of prominence in this history.

A Period of Experimenting

A new era may be said to have commenced in the early part of the seventies when we find Amédèe Bollèe exhibiting a steam machine at the Vienna Exposition. In the seventies were also experiments on modified forms of power on vehicle propelling motors other than steam, but it still seemed to be the steam vehicle that characterized the new period of activity which blossomed out in the early eighties with many ardent advocates, and exhibited a type of light vehicle with efficient strong boiler and light engine. America should not be overlooked, however, when we consider the one small vehicle of Austin, which was constructed in Massachusetts, and attracted great attention at the shows of the Ocean Circus, in the early seventies, or thereabout. Bouton, of France, came to the fore in the early eighties, and the light steam vehicle seemed on the high road to a great development and a monopoly of the common roads vehicle industry, until its competitor appeared in what is now popularly known as the gasoline vehicle in the middle eighties.

THE SELDEN PATENT

From this time on the great industry of to-day advanced in strides and jumps, but while the future had been anticipated in some suggestions and experiments in Europe, at last one great mind had delved into the problem and anticipated the great future of the new type of vehicle in America. Selden, after a decade or more of study and work, and well-directed experiments, had made his own deductions, and with clear discerning had concluded what, to his mind, would be *the* vehicle in the future. The result of his labors and the subsequent filing, in 1879, of a patent application, when considered in connection with his persistent work from that time on, even to the present day, would seem to justly mark him as the pioneer in this type of vehicle; in fact, he was so called by the Commissioner of Patents of the United States when publishing his annual report, immediately after the issue of Selden's patent.

ADVENT OF THE HYDRO-CARBON ENGINE

Then followed the work on carbureters and ignition devices and details of construction adapting the liquid hydro-carbons of uncertain quality to more satisfactory use. Details became and still are numerous, and optional to a great extent, but the liquid hydro-carbon engine of the compression type distinguished the new epoch. The development of the stationary engine operated with gas from receivers also proceeded rapidly in those days, though it was well into the eighties before the gas engine of the compression type involved a commercially successful industry to any extent; not for several years did the principal manufacturers take up commercially the proposition of the liquid hydro-carbon application. The development of the small engine using liquid hydro-carbons received attention from Marcus, in Austria, and the persistent attention of Benz and of Daimler, in Germany. The two latter, furthermore, adapted their engines to vehicles, and enthusiasm was great when Benz ran his three-wheeler, with explosive engine, through the streets of his native town.

Progress in France and America

England was still shackled; but in France many were inspired to change from steam to the hydro-carbon engine. About 1890 we find several French manufacturers procuring engines, or the right to manufacture the small explosive engines developed by the Germans, and promptly adapting them to their vehicle construction, already well developed for steam propulsion. Panhard & Levassor; Bouton, with his backer, DeDion; Bollèe, now Leon, the nephew; Delahaye and Peugeot, were among the earliest Frenchmen to appreciate the commercial possibilities of the new type. Then the large manufacturers, already experienced in other lines, and particularly in cycle manufacture, entered the field in 1893, 1894 and 1895; among them such old concerns as DeDetrich, manufacturers for one hundred and more years, grasped the opportunity. America was not idle, and while road conditions in this country militated largely against the early attempts in the industry, the efforts of the Duryeas and of Haynes, and various other experimenters, who have since retired, were heard from. It was difficult, however, with the obstacles then existing in America, for these early workers to secure encouragement, and progress was slow, just as the endeavors of Selden and some of the early steam vehicle people had received nothing but discouragement at the hands of those whom they endeavored to lead to the success of large manufacturing undertakings.

However, the Times-Herald race, in Chicago, near the close of 1895, brought forth a large number of inventors and several starters, including electric, steam and gasoline vehicles, and the showing was such as to practically satisfy the doubting that these were the beginning of the industry in this country.

The English Revival

Abroad, the leaders in the automobile movement organized the now historic races from Paris in different directions. With the runs of 1894, 1895 and 1896, and in each successive year thereafter, and with the road and other conditions improved, the industry rapidly developed. England also was at last reached. The restraints that had existed there for more than half a century could no more be endured. The burden was finally thrown off, for which great credit is due to Sir David Salomon, and the offensive Locomotive Act was at last repealed in August, 1896. The subsequent Locomotive Act which came into effect November 14, 1896, marked a red-letter day in motoring history for England, and was justly celebrated by a procession of vehicles from London to Brighton. Salomon had previously organized an exhibition in England, and had imported a French car, and as a prominent member of scientific and technical societies, in which he presented many papers on the subject, had done, possibly, more than any other individual to influence public sentiment and to secure this new enactment. English manufacturers were not entirely unprepared for the change, and a great wave of interest and activity swept the country. Naturally this was followed by a reaction, but since then a counter-reaction has set in, resulting in the present grand development of that class of manufacturing in the British Isles.

The small steam vehicle of Whitney, and his contemporaries, the Stanleys in the United States, then came to the fore. Under energetic promotion thousands of small vehicles of that type were manufactured and put into use. These, in no small measure, became to the public at large the convincing object lesson of the practicability and possibilities of the small automobile for every-day use.

Modern Conditions

The Paris show of 1900 revealed a great forward step in the development of constructions, and the offer immediately thereafter of the James Gordon Bennett trophy of international racing gave to the automobile industry such an impetus as has seldom been the good fortune of any other art to receive. To-day the automobile has reached that stage of perfection where the question is no longer whether or not the vehicle will carry you to a certain place and back. Now it is only a question of the speed, absence of vibration, and sweetness of running the engine, absence of all noise, and other details of refinement. Vehicles are now of the Pullman type, luxurious to the extent of prices ranging into the thirties of thousands of dollars, while on the other hand, thousands of small vehicles, costing between five hundred and one thousand dollars, are annually made and sold.

The steam machine, after being practically succeeded by the gasoline, was again improved by the flash boiler. The main development of this new power was carried on by Serpollet, of France, and later, by Rollin T. White, in the United States, both whom have become most able competitors of manufacturers of machines of other classes.

The Industry To-Day

The beginning of 1905 finds us with the annual shows, which have been consecutive for many years, while the census of vehicles now in use, or made in the last ten years, will aggregate several hundred thousand. The annual production is estimated as probably approximating one hundred thousand in a few of the principal countries. The value of the electrical vehicle, particularly as the town vehicle for anything except speeding, is now well established, and reports from Paris as well as New York indicate the lack of facilities of factories in this line for producing these carriages as rapidly as demanded. Heavy 'buses and individual vehicles alike are also popular.

PIONEER INVENTORS

PIONEER INVENTORS

Nicholas Joseph Cugnot,
William Murdock,
Oliver Evans,
William Symington,
Nathan Read,
Richard Trevithick,
David Gordon,
W. H. James,
Goldsworthy Gurney,
Thomas Blanchard,
M. Johnson,
Walter Hancock,
W. T. James,
Francis Maceroni,
Richard Roberts,
J. Scott Russell,
W. H. Church,
Etienne Lenoir,
Amédèe Bollèe,
George B. Selden,
Siegfried Marcus,
Carl Benz,
Gottlieb Daimler,
M. Levassor,
Leon Serpollet.

Nicholas Joseph Cugnot

Born at Void, Lorraine, France, September 25, 1725. Died in Paris, October 2, 1804.

Concerning the early life of Cugnot, little is known. He was educated for the engineering service of the French army, and gained distinction as a military and mechanical engineer. He also served as a military engineer in Germany. Soon afterward he entered the service of Prince Charles of Lorraine, and for a time resided at Brussels, where he gave lessons in the military art. He did not return to his native land until 1763, and then invented a new gun, with which the cavalry were equipped.

This brought him to the attention of the Compte de Saxe, and under the patronage of that nobleman, he constructed in 1765 his first locomotive. This was a small wagon. On its first run it carried four persons, and traveled at the rate of two and a quarter miles an hour. The boiler, however, being too small, the carriage could go only for fifteen or twenty minutes before the steam was exhausted, and it was necessary to stop the engine for nearly the same time, to enable the boiler to raise the steam to the maximum pressure, before it could proceed on its journey. This machine was a disappointment, in consequence of the inefficiency of the feed pumps. It has been stated that while in Brussels he had made a smaller vehicle, which, if so, was soon after 1760.

Several small accidents happened during the trial, for the machine could not be completely controlled, but it was considered on the whole to be fairly successful and worthy of further attention. The suggestion was made that provided it could be made more powerful, and its mechanism improved, it might be used to drag cannon into the field instead of using horses for that purpose. Consequently, Cugnot was ordered by the Duc de Choiseul, Minister of War, to proceed with the construction of an improved and more powerful machine. This vehicle, which was finished in 1770, cost twenty thousand livres. It was in two parts, a wagon and an engine. The wagon was carried on two wheels and had a seat for the steersman; the engine and boiler were supported on a single driving-wheel in front of the wagon. The two parts were united by a movable pin. A toothed quadrant, fixed on the framing of the fore part, was actuated by spur gearing on the upright steersman's shaft in close proximity to the seat, by means of which the conductor could cause the carriage to turn in either direction, at an angle of from fifteen to twenty degrees. In front was a round copper boiler, having a furnace inside, two small chimneys, two single-acting brass cylinders communicating with the boiler by the steam pipe, and other machinery. On each side of the driving-wheel, ratchet wheels were fixed, and as one of the pistons descended, the piston-rod drew a crank, the pawl of which, working into the ratchet-wheel, caused the driving-wheel to make a quarter of a revolution. By gearing, the same movement placed the piston on the other side in a position for making a stroke, and turned the four-way cock, so as to open the second cylinder to the steam and the first cylinder to the atmosphere. The second piston then descended, causing the leading wheel to make another quarter of a revolution, and restoring the first piston to its original position. In order to run the vehicle backwards, the pawl was made to act on the upper side, changing the position of the spring which pressed upon it; then, when the engine was started, the pawl caused the driving-wheel to turn a quarter of a revolution in the opposite direction with every stroke of the piston.

This machine was first tried in 1770 in the presence of a distinguished assembly, that included the Duc de Choiseul; General Gribeauval, First Inspector-General of Artillery; the Compte de Saxe, and others. Subsequently, other trials of it were made, with satisfactory results generally. The heavy over-balancing weight of the engine and boiler in front rendered it difficult to control. On one of its trips it ran into a wall in turning a corner and was partly wrecked. Further experiments with it were abandoned, and in 1800 it was deposited in the Conservatoire des Arts et Metier, Paris, where it still remains.

At a later period of his life, having lost his means of support, Cugnot's public services were considered to entitle him to a reward from the State. Louis Fifteenth gave him a pension of six hundred livres, but the French Revolution coming on, he was deprived even of that pittance, and he lived in abject misery in Brussels. His carriage was then in the arsenal, and a revolutionary committee, during the reign of terror, tried to take it out and reduce it to scrap, but was driven off. When Napoleon came to the throne, he restored the pension and increased it to one thousand livres. In addition to his inventions, Cugnot wrote several works on military art and fortification.

WILLIAM MURDOCK

Born in Bellow Mill, near Old Cumnock, Ayrshire, Scotland, August 21, 1754. Died at Sycamore Hill, November 15, 1839.

Murdock was the son of John Murdoch, a millwright. He was modestly educated, and brought up to his father's trade, helping to build and put up mill machinery. A curious production of the father and son, at this period, was a wooden horse, worked by mechanical power, on which young Murdock traveled about the country. When he was twenty-three years of age he entered the employment of the famous engineering firm of Boulton & Watt, at Soho, and there remained throughout his active life.

Watt recognized in him a valuable assistant, and his services were jealously regarded. On his part he devoted himself unreservedly to the interests of his employers. In 1777 he was sent to Cornwall to look after the pumps and engines set up by the firm in the mines, and for a long period he lived at Redruth. For some five years after 1800 he was engineer and superintendent at the Soho foundry. While living at Redruth, in 1792, he began a series of experiments on the illuminating properties of the gases of coal, wood, peat, and other substances, and in 1799 put up a gas-making apparatus at Soho. In 1803 he fitted the Soho factory with a gas-lighting system. Other inventions that are credited to him are models for an oscillating engine and a rotary engine, a method of making steam pipes, an apparatus for utilizing the force of compressed air, and a steam gun.

His early training and all his surroundings naturally and inevitably interested Murdock in the subject of steam locomotion, and before 1784 he began to experiment on these lines. That he made definite progress is shown in a letter that Thomas Wilson, agent in Cornwall of Boulton & Watt, wrote to his employers in August, 1786, saying, "William Murdock desires me to inform you that he has made a small engine of three-quarter-inch diameter and one and one-half inch stroke, that he has applied to a small carriage, which answers amazingly." He had made and run this model in 1784, and it is still in existence, and in the possession of the Messrs. Richard and George Tangye, England.

This model was on the high-pressure principle, and ran on three wheels, the single front one for steering. The vertical boiler, nearly over the rear axle, was heated by a spirit-lamp, and the machine stood only a little more than a foot high. The axle was cranked in the middle and turned by a rod connected to a beam moved up and down by the piston-rod projecting from the top of the cylinder. Yet it developed considerable speed. It is interesting to note that the use of the crank for converting the reciprocating motion of the steam engine into rotary was patented by Pickard in 1780, and Murdock's was probably its first application to self-propelled carriages.

The first experiment with this little engine was made in Murdock's house at Redruth, when the locomotive successfully hauled a wagon round the room, the single wheel, placed in front of the engine, fixed in such a position as to enable it to run round a circle.

Dr. Smiles, in his work on inventors, tells an amusing story concerning this machine. He says:

"Another experiment was made out of doors, on which occasion, small though the engine was, it fairly outran the speed of its inventor. One night, after returning from his duties at the mine at Redruth, Murdock went with his model locomotive to the avenue leading to the church, about a mile from the town. The walk was narrow, straight and level. Having lit the lamp, the water soon boiled, and off started the engine with the inventor after it. Shortly after he heard distant shouts of terror. It was too dark to perceive objects, but he found, on following up the machine, that the cries had proceeded from the worthy vicar, who, while going along the walk, had met the hissing and fiery little monster, which he declared he took to be the Evil One in propria persona!"

But Murdock was too useful a man to Boulton & Watt to be allowed to have free rein, and his inclination toward steam locomotion invention was apparently curbed, though it would appear Watt thought the roads of that time an insurmountable obstacle to the development of road vehicles, and wanted Murdock to devote his time to mechanical matters more ripe for success. Boulton, writing to Watt from Truro, in September, 1796, tells how he met Murdock on his way to London to get a patent on a new model, and how he persuaded him to turn back. This model was for a steam carriage that was afterward shown as able to travel freely around a room with a light load of shovel, poker and tongs upon it. His was probably the first high-pressure steam-engine vehicle run in England. Though only a small model, it did its proportionate work well.

Watt continued to oppose Murdock's scheme, but on one occasion suggested that he should be allowed an advance of five hundred dollars to enable him to prosecute his experiments, and if he succeeded within a year in making an engine capable of drawing a post chaise, carrying two passengers and the driver, at four miles an hour, it was suggested that he should be taken as partner into the locomotive business, for which Boulton and Watt were to provide the necessary capital. This proposition was never carried out. Again, in 1786, Watt said: "I wish William could be brought to do as we do, to mind the business in hand, and let such as Symington and Sadler throw away their time and money in hunting shadows." Murdock continued to speculate about steam locomotion on common roads, but never carried his ideas further. He retired from the employment of Boulton & Watt in 1830, and practically retired from all work at the same time.

Murdock seems to have had a very clear idea of the possibilities of steam propulsion on the common roads. Had circumstances permitted he might well have been expected to have solved the problem in 1796 quite as completely as his successors did in 1835. But he was a quarter of a century ahead of the time. Even the moderate public interest that existed later on had not manifested itself at all in his day and the condition of the English highways offered almost insuperable obstacles to steam vehicular travel. Personally his lack of self-assertiveness and his feeling of dependence upon Boulton and Watt also held him back. So he remained simply one of the pioneer investigators pointing the way for others.

Oliver Evans

Born in 1755 or 1756, in Newport, Del. Died in Philadelphia, April 21, 1819.

Little has been preserved respecting the early history of Oliver Evans, who has been aptly styled "The Watt of America." His parents were farming people, and he had only an ordinary common-school education. At the age of fourteen he was apprenticed to a wheelwright or wagonmaker, and continued his meager education by studying at night time by the light that he made by burning chips and shavings in the fireplace.

While yet an apprentice his attention was turned to the subject of propelling land carriages without animal power. But the lack of definite knowledge in regard to steam power compelled him to abandon his plans, although his experiments were continued for a long time. Soon after attaining his majority he was engaged in making card-teeth by hand, and in connection therewith developed several labor-saving improvements. He also invented improvements in the construction of machinery of flour mills that effected a complete revolution in the manufacture of flour. These improvements consisted of the elevator, the conveyor, the hopper-boy, the drill and the descender, which various machines were applied in different mills so as to perform mechanically every necessary movement of the grain and meal from one part of the mill to the other, causing a saving of fully one-half in the labor of mill attendance and manufacturing the flour better. These improvements were not accepted by the mill owners at the outset, and Evans spent many discouraging years before he could finally persuade the manufacturers of the utility of his inventions. In the end, however, he lived to see his inventions generally introduced, and he profited largely thereby.

In the year 1786, Evans petitioned the Legislature of Pennsylvania for the exclusive right to use his improvements in flour mills and steam carriages in that State, and in the year following presented a similar petition to the Legislature of Maryland. In the former instance he was only successful so far as to obtain the privilege of the mill improvements, his representations concerning steam carriages being considered as savoring too much of insanity to deserve notice. He was more fortunate in Maryland, for, although the steam project was laughed at, yet one of his friends, a member, very judiciously observed that the grant could injure no one, for he did not think that any man in the world had thought of such a thing before, and therefore he wished the encouragement might be afforded, as there was a prospect that it would produce something useful. This kind of argument had its effect, and Evans received all that he asked for, and from that period considered himself bound in honor to the State of Maryland to produce a steam carriage, as soon as his means would allow him.

For several years succeeding the granting of his petition by the Legislature of Maryland, Evans endeavored to obtain some person of pecuniary resources to join with him in his plans; and for this purpose explained his views by drafts, and otherwise, to some of the first mechanics in the country. Although the persons addressed appeared, in several instances, to understand them, they declined any assistance from a fear of the expense and difficulty of their execution.

In the year 1800, or 1801, Evans, never having found anyone willing to contribute to the expense, or even to encourage him in his efforts, determined to construct a steam carriage at his own expense. Previous to commencing he explained his views to Robert Patterson, Professor of Mathematics in the University of Pennsylvania, and to an eminent English engineer. They both declared the principles new to them, and advised the plan as highly worthy of a fair experiment. They were the only persons who had any confidence, or afforded encouraging advice. He also communicated his plans to B. F. Latrobe, the scientist, who publicly pronounced them as chimerical, and attempted to demonstrate the absurdity of Evans' principles in his report to the Philosophical Society of Pennsylvania on steam engines. In this he also endeavored to show the impossibility of making steamboats useful.

Evans commenced and had made considerable progress in the construction of a steam carriage, when the idea occurred to him that as his steam engine was altogether different in form, as well as in principle, from any other in use, a patent could be obtained for it, and then applied to mills more profitably than to carriages. The steam carriage was accordingly laid aside for a season of more leisure, and the construction of a small engine was commenced, with a cylinder six inches in diameter and a piston of eighteen inches stroke, for a mill to grind plaster of paris. The expense of its construction far exceeded Evans' calculation, and before the engine was finished he found it cost him all he was worth. He had then to begin the world anew, at the age of forty-eight, with a large family to support, and that, too, with a knowledge that if the trial failed his credit would be entirely ruined, and his prospects for the remainder of life dark and gloomy. But fortune favored him, and his success was complete.

In a brief account, given by himself, of his experiments in steam, he says: "I could break and grind three hundred bushels of plaster of paris, or twelve tons, in twenty-four hours; and to show its operations more fully to the public, I applied it to saw stone, on the side of Market Street, where the driving of twelve saws in heavy frames, sawing at the rate of one hundred feet of marble in twelve hours, made a great show and excited much attention. I thought this was sufficient to convince the thousands of spectators of the utility of my discovery, but I frequently heard them inquire if the power could be applied to saw timber as well as stone, to grind grain, propel boats, etc., and though I answered in the affirmative, they still doubted. I therefore determined to apply my engine to all new uses; to introduce it and them to the public. This experiment completely tested the correctness of my principles. The power of my engine rises in a geometrical proportion, while the consumption of the fuel has only an arithmetical ratio; in such proportion that every time I added one-fourth more to the consumption of the fuel, its powers were doubled; and that twice the quantity of fuel required to drive one saw, would drive sixteen saws at least; for when I drove two saws the consumption was eight bushels of coal in twelve hours, but when twelve saws were driven, the consumption was not more than ten bushels, so that the more we resist the steam, the greater is the effect of the engine. On these principles very light but powerful engines can be made suitable for propelling boats and land carriages without the great encumbrance of their weight as mentioned in Latrobe's demonstration."

In the year 1840, Evans, by order of the Board of Health of Philadelphia, constructed at his works, situated a mile and a half from the water, a machine for cleaning docks. It consisted of a large flat or scow, with a steam engine of five horse-power on board, to work the machinery to raise the mud into the scows. This was considered a fine opportunity to show the public that his engine could propel both land and water conveyances. When the machine was finished, he fixed, in a rough and temporary manner, wheels with wooden axletrees, and, of course, under the influence of great friction. Although the whole weight was equal to two hundred barrels of flour, yet his small engine propelled it up Market Street and round the circle to the water-works, where it was launched into the Schuylkill River. A paddle-wheel was then applied to its stern, and it thus moved down that river to the Delaware, a distance of sixteen miles, leaving behind all vessels that were under sail.

This demonstration was in the presence of thousands of spectators, which he supposed would have convinced them of the practicability of steamboats and steam carriages. But no allowance was made by the public for the disproportion of the engine to its load, nor for the rough manner in which the machinery was fixed, or the great friction and ill form of the boat, and it was supposed that this was the utmost it could perform. Some individuals undertook to ridicule the experiment of driving so great a weight on land, because the motion was too slow to be useful. The inventor silenced them by answering that he would make a carriage propelled by steam, for a wager of three thousand dollars, to run upon a level road, against the swiftest horse that could be produced. This machine Evans named the Oructor Amphibolis.

On the 25th of September, 1804, Evans submitted to the consideration of the Lancaster Turnpike Company a statement of the costs and profits of a steam carriage to carry one hundred barrels of flour, fifty miles in twenty-four hours; tending to show that one such steam carriage would make more net profits than ten wagons, drawn by five horses each, on a good turnpike road, and offering to build one at a very low price. His address closed as follows: "It is too much for an individual to put in operation every improvement which he may invent. I have no doubt but that my engines will propel boats against the current of the Mississippi, and wagons on turnpike roads, with great profit. I now call upon those whose interest it is to carry this invention into effect. All of which is respectfully submitted to your consideration." Little or no attention was paid to this offer, for it was difficult at that day to interest anyone in steam locomotion.

Evans' interest in the steam carriage forthwith ceased, but in his writings, published about that time, he remarked: "The time will come when people will travel in stages moved by steam engines from one city to another, almost as fast as birds fly, fifteen or twenty miles an hour. Passing through the air with such velocity, changing the scene in such rapid succession, will be the most rapid exhilarating exercise. A carriage (steam) will set out from Washington in the morning, the passengers will breakfast at Baltimore, dine at Philadelphia, and sup at New York in the same day." To accomplish this he suggested railways of wood or iron, or smooth paths of broken stone or gravel, and predicted that engines would soon drive boats ten or twelve miles an hour. In the latter years of his life, Evans established a large iron foundry in Philadelphia.

Although Evans' distinct contribution to the problem of steam locomotion on the common roads was not particularly practical it was at least important as being the first suggestion of anything of the kind in the United States. Road conditions in this country at that time were worse than they were in England and yet under more discouraging circumstances he was as far advanced in ideas and plans as his great contemporaries, Trevithick and others across the water. To Evans must be given the credit of perfecting the high-pressure, non-condensing engine, and even Trevithick, "the father of the locomotive," was largely indebted to him for his progress in the lines he was working on in England, his plans and specifications having been sent abroad for the English engineers to inspect in 1784.

William Symington

Born at Leadhills, Scotland, October, 1783. Died in London, March 22, 1831.

More fortunate than most of the English inventors of the seventeenth and eighteenth centuries, with whom he was associated, William Symington came of a family that was able to give him a good education. His father was a mechanic who had charge of the engines and machinery at the Warlockhead lead mines, and the son gained his first knowledge of mechanics and engineering in the shops with his father. Intended for the ministry, he was sent to the University of Glasgow and the University of Dublin to pursue his studies. But the ministry had slight attractions for him, and when the time came for him to choose a profession, he adopted that of civil engineering.

In 1786 he worked out a model for a steam road-car. This was regarded very highly by all who saw it. It is said that Mr. Meason, manager of the lead mines at Warlockhead, was so pleased with the model, the merit of which principally belonged to young Symington, that he sent him into Edinburgh for the purpose of exhibiting it before the professors of the University, and other scientific gentlemen of the city, in the hope that it might lead in some way to his future advancement in life. Mr. Meason became the patron and friend of Symington, allowed the model to be exhibited at his own house, and invited many persons of distinction to inspect it. The carriage supported on four wheels had a locomotive behind, the front wheels being arranged with steering-gear. A cylindrical boiler was used for generating steam, which communicated by a steam-pipe with the two horizontal cylinders, one on each side of the firebox of the boiler. When steam was turned into the cylinder, the piston made an outward stroke; a vacuum was then formed, the steam being condensed in a cold water tank placed beneath the cylinders, and the piston was forced back by the pressure of the atmosphere. The piston rods communicated their motion to the driving-axle and wheels through rack rods, which worked toothed wheels placed on the hind axle on both sides of the engine, and the alternate action of the rack rods upon the tooth and ratchet wheels, with which the drums were provided, produced the rotary motion. The boiler was fitted with a lever and weight safety valve. Symington's locomotive was abandoned, the inventor considering that the scheme of steam travel on the common roads was impracticable.

Henceforth, Symington gave his attention to the study of boat propulsion by steam. In 1787 he got out a patent for an improved form of steam engine, in which he obtained rotary action by chains and ratchet-wheels. This engine, with a four-inch cylinder, was used to work the paddles of a pleasure boat on Dalswinton Loch, in 1788, the boat steaming at the rate of five miles an hour. This boat is now in the South Kensington Museum, and it has been termed "the parent engine of steam navigation." The experiment with this method of boat propulsion was so successful that a year later larger engines, with eighteen-inch cylinders, were fitted to another boat, which attained a speed of seven miles an hour. In 1801, Symington took out a patent for an engine with a piston rod guided by rollers in a straight path and connected by a rod with a crank attached directly to the paddle-wheel shaft—the system that has been in use ever since. Although the perfect practicability of this method of boat propulsion was fully demonstrated by a trial on the tug-boat Charlotte Dundas, in March, 1802, the plan for steam power on canals and lakes was not carried further. The Forth and Clyde Company, and the Duke of Bridgewater, who were backing Symington, gave up the project and he could get help from no other sources. His inventions and experiments are generally regarded as marking the beginning of steam navigation. It is interesting to note that among those who were guests on the Charlotte Dundas, on the occasion of this trial trip, was Robert Fulton, who wrote a treatise on steam navigation in 1793, tried a small steamboat on the river Seine, in France, in 1803, and in 1807 launched his famous steamship, the Clermont, on the Hudson River.

Symington, disappointed and discouraged, gave up his work and went to London. The rest of his life was for the most part thrown away, and he became one of the waifs and strays of London. In 1825 he received a grant of one hundred pounds from the privy purse, and later on fifty pounds more, in recognition of his services for steam navigation. He died in obscurity and although he was unquestionably the pioneer in his country of the successful application of steam to navigation on inland waters his name is only a bare memory.

NATHAN READ

Born in Warren, Mass., July 2, 1759. Died near Belfast, Me., January 20, 1849.

Graduated from Harvard College in 1781, Read was a tutor at Harvard for four years. In 1788 he began experimenting to discover some way of utilizing the steam engine for propelling boats and carriages. His efforts were mainly directed toward devising lighter, more compact machinery than then generally in use. His greatest invention at that time was a substitute for the large working-beam. This was a cross-head beam which ran in guides and had a connecting-rod with which motion was communicated. The new cylinder that he invented to attach to this working-frame was double-acting. In order to make the boiler more portable he invented a multitubular form, and this he patented, together with the cylinder, chain-wheel, and other appliances.

The boiler was cylindrical and was placed upright or horizontal, and the furnace was carried within it. A double cylinder formed a water-jacket, connected with a water and steam chamber above, and a water-chamber below. Numerous small straight tubes connected these two chambers. Read also invented another boiler in which the fire went through small spiral tubes, very much as it does in the present-day locomotives, and this was a smoke-consuming engine. For the purpose of acquiring motion he first used paddle-wheels, but afterward adopted a chain-wheel of his own invention.

Read planned a steam-car to be run with his tubular boiler, and it is said that this vehicle, when laden with fifty tons weight, could make five miles per hour. The model which was completed in 1790 had four wheels, the front pair being pivoted at the center and controlled by a horizontal sheave and rope. The sheave was located back near the boiler, and in guiding the machine it was operated by a hand-wheel placed above the platform, within easy reach of the engineer. A square boiler with Read's multi-tubular system, overhung at the rear of the carriage. Two driving-wheels were forward of the boiler, and in front of these were two horizontal cylinders on each side of the engine. On the inside of each wheel were ratched teeth that fitted into corresponding teeth on horizontal racks above and below the hub. The piston, moving back and forth from the cylinder, engaged these teeth and caused a revolution of the wheel. There were two steam valves and two exhaust valves to each cylinder, the exhaust being into the atmosphere. Although this was the first conception of propulsion by steam on land in America, Read went no further in creating this model, inasmuch as he received no encouragement from financial sources.

In 1796, Read established at Salem, Mass., the Salem Iron Foundry, where he manufactured anchors, chain cables, and other machinery. In January, 1798, he invented a machine to cut and head nails at one operation. He also invented a method of equalizing the action of windmills by accumulating the force of the wind through winding up a weight; and a plan for harnessing the force of the tides by means of reservoirs which, by being alternately filled up and emptied, created a constant stream of water. Among his other inventions were a pumping engine and a threshing machine.

RICHARD TREVITHICK

Born in Illogan, in the west of Cornwall, England, April 13, 1771. Died in Dartford, Kent, April 22, 1833.

Richard Trevithick had meager educational advantages. His father was manager of the Dolcoath and other mines, and shortly after the birth of his son moved to Penponds, near Camborne, where the boy was sent to school to learn reading, writing and arithmetic, which were the limits of his attainments. Early in life he showed the dawning of remarkable inventive genius, was quick at figures and clever in drawing. He developed into a young man of notable physique, being six feet two inches high, and having the frame and the strength of an athlete. He was one of the most powerful wrestlers in the west country, and it is related of him that he could easily lift a thousand-weight mandril.

At the age of eighteen young Trevithick began to assist his father as mine manager, and at once proceeded to put his inventive faculty to practical test. His initial success, in 1795, was an improvement upon an engine at the Wheal Treasury mine, which accomplished a great saving in fuel and in power, and won for him his first royalty. Before his father died, in 1797, he had attained to the position of engineer at the Ding Dong mine, near Penzance, and had already set up at the Herland mine the engine built by William Bull, with improvements of his own. His earliest invention of importance was in 1797, when he made an improved plunger pump, which, in the following year, he developed into a double-acting water-pressure engine. One of these engines, set up in 1804, at the Alport mine, in Derbyshire, was run until 1850.

In 1780 he built a double-acting high-pressure engine with a crank, for Cook's Kitchen mine. This was known as the Puffer, from the noise that it made, and it soon came into general use in Cornwall and South Wales, a successful rival of the low-pressure steam vacuum engine of Watt.

As early as 1796 Trevithick began to give attention to the subject of steam locomotion, and a model constructed by him before 1800 is now in the South Kensington Museum. He busied himself in designing and building a steam vehicle to travel upon the common highways. The work was done in a workshop at Camborne, and some of it in the shop of Captain Andrew Vivian. It was Christmas Eve of 1801 when this steam locomotive was completed and was brought out for trial.

The following account of the first trial was made by one who was present: "I knew Captain Dick Trevithick very well. I was a cooper by trade, and when Trevithick was making his steam carriage I used to go every day into John Tyack's shop at the Weith, close by here, where they put her together. In the year 1801, upon Christmas Eve, towards night, Trevithick got up steam, out on the high road, just outside the shop. When we saw that Trevithick was going to turn on steam, we jumped up, as many as could, maybe seven or eight of us. 'Twas a stiffish hill going up to Camborne Beacon, but she went off like a little bird. When she had gone about a quarter of a mile there was a rough piece of road covered with loose stones. She didn't go quite so fast, and as it was a flood of rain, and we were very much squeezed together, I jumped off. She was going faster than I could walk, and went up the hill about half a mile further, when they turned her and came back again to the shop." The next day the engine steamed to Captain Vivian's house, and a few days subsequently, Trevithick and Vivian started off for Tehidy House, where Lord Dedunstanville lived, some two or three miles from Camborne. On this journey they met with an accident, the engine being overturned in going around a curve; but they got back safely.

This carriage presented the appearance of an ordinary stage coach on four wheels. The engine had one horizontal cylinder which, together with the boiler and the furnace-box, was placed in the rear of the hind axle. The motion of the piston was transmitted to a separate crank-axle, from which, through the medium of spur-gear, the axle of the driving-wheel, which was mounted with a fly-wheel, derived its motion. The steam cocks and the force-pump, as also the bellows used for the purpose of quickening combustion in the furnace, were worked off the same crank axle. This was one of the first successful high-pressure engines constructed on the principle of moving a piston by the elasticity of steam against the pressure only of the outside atmosphere.

In the following year Trevithick went to London with his cousin, Andrew Vivian, and secured a patent. Early in 1803 he made his second steam carriage. This was built at Camborne and taken to London, via Plymouth, for exhibition. Its journey along the highways thoroughly alarmed the country people. Coleridge relates that a toll-gate keeper was so frightened at the appearance of the sputtering, smoke-spitting thing of fearsome mien that, trembling in every limb and with teeth chattering, he threw aside the toll-gate with the scared exclamation, "No—noth—nothing to pay. My de—dear Mr. Devil, do drive on as fast as you can. Nothing to pay!"

The engine in this carriage had a cylinder five and one-half inches in diameter, with a stroke of two and one-half feet, and with thirty pounds of steam it worked five strokes per minute. In every way it was superior to its predecessor. It was not so heavy; and the horizontal cylinder, instead of the vertical, added very much to its steadiness of motion; while wheels of a larger diameter enabled it the more easily to pass over rough roads which had brought the Camborne one to a standstill. The boiler was made entirely of wrought iron, and the cylinder was inserted horizontally, close behind the driving axle. A forked piston-rod was used, the ends working in guides, so that the crank axle might be brought near to the cylinder. Spur gearing and couplings were used on each side of the carriage for communicating motion from the crank shaft to the main driving axle. The driving-wheels were about ten feet diameter, and made of wood. The framing was of wrought iron. The coach was intended to seat eight or ten persons, and the greater part of the weight came on the driving axle. The coach was suspended upon springs.

The London steam carriage was put together at Felton's carriage shop, in Leather Lane, and after its completion, Vivian one day ran the locomotive from Leather Lane, Gray's Inn Lane, on to Lords' Cricket Ground, to Paddington, and home again by way of Islington, a journey of ten miles through the streets of London. Several trips were made in Tottenham Court Road and Euston Square, and only once did they meet with accident. Finally, however, the frame of the carriage got twisted, and the engine was detached and set to driving a mill.

Trevithick's next experiment was made in 1803-4, while he was engineer of the Pen-y-darran iron works, near Merthyr Tydvil, where he built and ran on a railway a locomotive that was fairly successful. In 1808 he built a locomotive for a circular railway or steam circus that he and Andrew Vivian set up in London, near Euston Square. This ran for several weeks, carrying passengers at the rate of twelve or fifteen miles an hour around curves of fifty or one hundred feet radius. One day a rail broke and the engine was overturned, which ended the exhibition.

Subsequently, Trevithick applied his high-pressure engine to rock-boring and breaking, and dredging. He laid out a system of dredging the Thames River, planned a tunnel under the Thames, invented a high-pressure steam threshing engine in 1812, constructed iron tanks and buoys, and modeled an iron ship. He was one of the first to conceive the practical use of steam in agriculture, declaring that the use of the steam engine for this purpose would "double the population of the kingdom and make our markets the cheapest in the world."

In 1814, Trevithick became interested in a plan to work the silver mines of Peru by Cornish methods, and nine of his high-pressure engines were sent to South America in charge of Henry Vivian and other engineers. He himself followed in 1816, and remained in that country ten years, making and losing several fortunes during that time. Finally, in a revolution, the mining plants were destroyed, and he was forced to leave the country, penniless. For a time he was prospecting in Costa Rica, where he planned a railroad across the Isthmus from the Atlantic to the Pacific. In 1827 he returned to England, still a poor man, and settling in Dartford, Kent, devoted himself to new inventions, unsuccessfully endeavoring to secure the help of the government in his work. His later years were spent in poverty, and when he died, the expense of his burial was borne by his fellow-workmen of Dartford.

Undoubtedly, Trevithick was one of the foremost English engineers of his day, a period that was rich with strong men of distinction in his profession. By many he has been considered as having contributed more even than James Watt to the development of the steam engine and its broader adaptation to practical uses. In his early years he was restrained in putting his ideas and experiments to practical test by the restrictions of Watt's patents. Finally when that difficulty was removed he at once took a leading position in his profession. Especially in the development of the high pressure engine he is entitled to at least as much credit as any man of his day. His genius was fully recognized in his generation and his impoverished old age was the result of financial reverses in business operations and not from the lack of substantial rewards for his inventive achievements.

David Gordon

The first experiments of David Gordon, who in 1819 was working with William Murdock, in Soho, were for the purpose of using compressed air for common road locomotives. He also invented a portable gas apparatus, and originated a society of gentlemen, with the intention of forming a company for the purpose of running a mail coach and other carriages by means of a high-pressure engine, or of a gas vacuum or pneumatic engine, supplied with portable gas. Alexander Gordon, his son, states that "the committee of the society had only a limited sum at their disposal, nor were there to be more funds until a carriage had been propelled for a considerable distance at the rate of ten miles an hour." David Gordon then tried to prevail upon the committee to make use of a steam engine, but evidently without success.

In 1821 he took out a patent for improvements in wheel carriages, and his locomotive is fully described in the interesting Treatise on Elemental Locomotion, by Mr. Alexander Gordon. The machine consisted of a large hollow cylinder about nine feet in diameter and five long, having its internal circumference provided with a continuous series of cogged teeth, into which were made to work the cogged running wheels of a locomotive steam engine, similar to that of Trevithick. The steam power being communicated to the wheels of the carriage, caused them to revolve, and to climb up the internal rack of the large cylinder. The center of gravity of the engine being thus constantly made to change its position, and to throw its chief weight on the forward side of the axis of the cylinder, the latter was compelled to roll forward, propelling the vehicle before it, and whatever train might be added.

Gordon's next attempt to construct locomotive carriages for the common road was in 1824. The means proposed was a modification of the method invented by William Brunton. But instead of the propellers being operated upon by the alternating motion of the piston-rod, as in Brunton's vehicle, Gordon contrived to give them a continuous rotatory action and to apply the force of the engines in a more direct manner. The carriage ran upon three wheels, one in the front to steer by, and two behind to bear the chief weight. Each of the wheels had a separate axle, the ends of which had their bearings upon parallel bars, the wheels rolling in a perpendicular position. This arrangement, by avoiding the usual cross-axle, afforded an increased uninterrupted space in the body of the vehicle.

In the fore part of the carriage were placed the steam engines, consisting of two brass cylinders, in a horizontal position, but vibrating upon trunnions. The piston-rods of these engines gave motion to an eight-throw crank, two in the middle for the cylinders, and three on each side, to which were attached the propellers; by the revolution of the crank, these propellers or legs were successively forced outwards, with the feet of each against the ground in a backward direction, and were immediately afterwards lifted from the ground by the revolution of another crank, parallel to the former, and situated at a proper distance from it on the same frame. The propelling-rods were formed of iron gas-tubes, filled with wood, to combine lightness with strength. To the lower ends of these propelling-rods were attached the feet, in the form of segments of circles, and made on their under side like a short and very stiff brush of whalebone, supported by intermixed iron teeth, to take effect in case the whalebone failed. These feet pressed against the ground in regular succession, by a kind of rolling, circular motion, without digging it up. The guide had the power of lifting these legs off the ground at pleasure, so that in going down hill, when the gravity was sufficient for propulsion, nothing but a brake was put into requisition to retard the motion, if necessary. If the carriage was proceeding upon a level, the lifting of the propellers was equivalent to the subtraction of the power, and soon brought it to a full stop. When making turns in a road the guide had only to lift the propellers on one side of the carriage and allow the others to operate alone, until the curve was traversed.

Gordon got fair results from this locomotive, but the speed was not satisfactory. In his first trials he found the power insufficient. He afterwards fitted one of Gurney's light boilers in the hinder part of the carriage, though even after this improvement had been added the experiments were disappointing. Gordon was convinced that the application of the power to the wheels was the proper mode of propulsion, and his project was abandoned after six or seven years had been spent in inventing, constructing, and carrying out experiments with four distinct carriages.

William Henry James

Born at Henley, England, March, 1776. Died at Dulwich College Alms House, December 16, 1873.

The father of William Henry James was William James, of Warwickshire, the great railway projector of his time. He was a solicitor in early life, but became wealthy, worked a colliery in South Staffordshire, and in 1815 removed to London, where he had a large land agency business. He became interested in tramways in 1806, and from that date on devoted most of his energies and fortune to projecting railways in the United Kingdom. He had an interest in one of George Stephenson's patents, made numerous railway surveys, and by many has been considered to have done more than any single individual in laying the foundations of the English railroad system.

William Henry James assisted his father in his railway surveys in early life, and then began business independently as an engineer, in Birmingham. He made experiments in steam locomotion on common roads, and took out patents for locomotive steam engines, boilers, driving apparatus, and so on. His patent for a water-tube boiler for road locomotives was secured in 1823, and his first car was built in 1824. This was a twenty-passenger steam coach. Each rear wheel had a double-cylinder engine, and the pistons were worked at a pressure of two hundred pounds per square inch. Separate engines to each driver gave each wheel an independent motion, so that power and speed might be varied for turning corners, the outer wheel travelling over a much greater space than the inner wheel. When the front wheels were so placed that the carriage proceeded in a straight line an equal amount of steam was admitted to each pair of cylinders, but when the front wheel was in the lock the engine driving the outer wheel received a greater amount of steam and thus developed more power and traveled faster than the inner wheel. This arrangement was said to be so efficient that the carriage could be made to describe every variety of curve, repeatedly making turns of less than ten feet radius. The whole of the machinery was mounted upon laminated carriage springs. This arrangement caused the engines and their framework to vibrate altogether upon the crank-shaft as a center, at the same time connecting these engines to the boiler by means of hollow axles moving in stuffing boxes. Each engine had two cylinders of small diameter and long stroke; to these separate engines steam was supplied from the boiler by means of the main pipe, which moved through steam-tight stuffing boxes to the slide valve-boxes by small pipes. The locomotive was entirely distinct from the passenger carriage.

Sir James C. Anderson became associated with James, and in 1829 they built another carriage. This weighed nearly three tons, and the first trials were made round a circle of one hundred and sixty feet in diameter. When it was finally ready to be brought out it was loaded with fifteen passengers and driven several miles on a rough gravel road across Epping Forest, with a speed varying from twelve to fifteen miles an hour. Steam was supplied by two tubular boilers, each forming a hollow cylinder four feet six inches long. The tubes of which the boilers were composed were common gas pipe, one of which split on one of the trips, thus letting the water out of one of the boilers and extinguishing its fire. Under these circumstances, with only one boiler in operation, the carriage returned home at the rate of about seven miles an hour, carrying more than twenty passengers—at one period, indeed, it is said, a much greater number; showing that sufficient steam could be generated in such a boiler to be equal to the propulsion of between five and six tons weight. In consequence of this demonstration that the most brilliant success was attainable, the proprietors dismantled the carriage and commenced the construction of superior tubular boilers with much stronger tubes.

Shortly after Anderson and James commenced to build another steam carriage, which was ready for use in November, 1829. This engine was not intended to carry passengers, but to be employed for drawing carriages behind. Four tubular boilers were used, the total number of tubes being nearly two hundred. These boilers were enclosed in a space four feet wide, three feet long, and two feet deep. The steam from each boiler was conducted into one main steam pipe one and one-half inches in diameter, and the communication from any one of the boilers could be cut off in case of leakage. Four cylinders, each two and one-quarter inch bore and nine inch stroke, were arranged vertically in the hind part of the locomotive, and two of them acted upon each crank-shaft as before, giving a separate motion to each driving wheel.

The exhaust steam was conducted through two copper tanks for heating the feed water to a high temperature, and thence passed to the chimney. The steering-gear consisted of an external pillar containing a vertical shaft, at the upper end of which small bevel-gearing was used, giving motion to the vertical shaft, whose bottom end carried a pinion gearing into a sector attached to the fore axle. The motion of the crank-shafts was communicated to the separate axles of the driving-wheels by spur-gearing with two speeds.

In experiments made with this carriage, the greatest speed obtained upon a level, on a very indifferent road, was at the rate of fifteen miles an hour, and it never ran more than three or four miles without breaking some of the steam joints. The Mechanic's Magazine, reporting one of these trials, said: "A series of interesting experiments were made throughout the whole of yesterday with a new steam carriage belonging to Sir James Anderson, Bart., and W. H. James, Esq., on the Vauxhall, Kensington, and Clapham roads, with the view of ascertaining the practical advantages of some perfectly novel apparatus attached to the engines, the results of which were so satisfactory that the proprietors intend immediately establishing several stage coaches on the principle. The writer was favored with a ride during the last experiment, when the machine proceeded from Vauxhall Bridge to the Swan at Clapham, a distance of two and a half miles, which was run at the rate of fifteen miles an hour. From what I had the pleasure of witnessing, I am confident that this carriage is far superior to every other locomotive carriage hitherto brought before the public, and that she will easily perform fifteen miles an hour throughout a long journey. The body of the carriage, if not elegant, is neat, being the figure of a parallelogram. It is a very small and compact machine, and runs upon four wheels."

W. H. James patented another steam carriage in August, 1832. This varied much from his earlier engines in the working parts, and it was not generally considered to be as satisfactory as the others. Sir James Anderson was not able, for pecuniary reasons, to continue to back James in his experimenting, and it does not appear that these plans of 1832 were ever consummated in a completed vehicle.

James was a man of strong mind, an original thinker and thoroughly well-trained by his apprenticeship with his father. He spent a good part of his life in experimenting with common-road steam propulsion, but he had not monetary resources or financial ability commensurate with his mechanical genius. When the support of Anderson was withdrawn from him he seems to have been compelled to give up. Little has been recorded concerning the latter years of his life, and his death in the almshouse sufficiently indicates the poverty in which his last years were spent. His father also sacrificed his life to the cause of railroad advancement, losing his entire fortune and dying a poor man.

GOLDSWORTHY GURNEY

Born at Treator, near Padstow, Cornwall, England, February 14, 1793. Died at Reeds, near Bade, February 28, 1875.

The son of John Gurney, Goldsworthy Gurney received a good elementary education at the Truro Grammar School, and then studied medicine. He settled at Wadebridge as a surgeon, but although very successful, gradually turned his attention to scientific and mechanical investigations. He constructed an organ, studied chemistry and mechanical science, and removing to London in 1820, delivered a series of lectures on heat, electricity and gases at the Surrey Institute. His investigations resulted in the invention of the oxy-hydrogen blowpipe, and the discovery of the powerful lime-light known as the Drummond light, and he engaged in other experiments in this field of research.

In 1804, while on a holiday at Camborne, he saw a Trevithick engine on wheels. Recalling this in after years he began experimenting on steam locomotion in 1823, and soon abandoned his surgical and medical practice for this new pursuit. His first efforts were toward the construction of an engine to travel on the common roads. The weight of the steam engines that were then being built seemed to him to offer great objections to their use for this purpose, but he succeeded, with his first machine, in reducing weight from four tons to thirty hundredweight. Then he secured a sufficiency of power by the invention of the high-pressure steam jet. This invention differed from those of Stephenson and Trevithick, who sent their waste steam up through the chimney instead of utilizing it. The Gurney jet was applied to the Stephenson Rocket engine on the Liverpool and Manchester Railway, in October, 1829, and also to steamboats and steam carriages.

In 1823, Gurney made his first experiments with a model steam carriage, on which propellers or feet were used. Two years later, in 1825, he completed a full-size carriage on the same plan, and in May of that year he took out his first patent for this vehicle. The carriage was impelled by these legs being alternately drawn forwards and pressed backwards by a steam engine acting upon them through movable oblong blocks, to which they were attached. As a first experiment this carriage was driven up Windmill Hill, near Kilburn. Another trip, between London and Edgeware, demonstrated the inefficiency of these propellers, and led to the discovery that there was sufficient friction between wheels and the ground to insure propulsion.

In 1826 he constructed a coach about twenty feet long, which would accommodate six inside and fifteen outside passengers, besides the engineer. The driving-wheels were five feet diameter, and the leading wheels three feet nine inches diameter. Two propellers were used, which could be put in motion when the carriage was climbing hills. Gurney's patent boiler was used for supplying steam to the twelve horse-power engine. The total weight of the carriage was about a ton and a half. In front of the coach was a capacious boot, while behind, that which had the appearance of a boot, was the case for the boiler and the furnace, from which it was calculated that no inconvenience would be experienced by the outside passenger, although in cold weather a certain degree of heat might be obtained, if required. In descending a hill, there was a brake fixed on the hind wheel, to increase the friction; but, independently of this, the guide had the power of lessening the force of the steam to any extent by means of the lever at his right hand, which operated upon the throttle valve, and by which he could stop the action of the steam altogether and effect a counter vacuum in the cylinders. By this means also he regulated the rate of progress on the road. There was another lever by which he could stop the vehicle instantly, and in a moment reverse the motion of the wheels.

This carriage traveled up Highgate Hill to Edgeware, and also to Stanmore, and went up both Stanmore Hill and Brockley Hill. In ascending these hills the driving-wheels did not slip, so that the legs were not needed. After these experiments the propellers were removed.

Gurney obtained another patent in 1827, and under this worked a steam carriage resembling the common stage coach, with the boiler in the hind boot. This carriage was run experimentally to Barnet, Edgeware, Finchley, and other places, and in 1828 it was said that a trip was made from London to Melksham, thirteen miles from Bath, a distance of nearly two hundred miles. On the return trip the rate of speed was about twelve miles an hour.

Gurney's carriage so fully established its practicability, that in 1830, Sir Charles Dance contracted for several, and ran them successfully from London to Holyhead, and from Birmingham to Bristol. In the following year he ran over the turnpike road between Gloucester and Cheltenham for four months in succession, four times a day, without an accident or delay of consequence. The distance of nine miles was regularly covered in from forty-five to fifty-five minutes. Nearly three thousand persons were carried, and nearly four thousand miles traveled.

A strong public sentiment against the use of the common roads by these vehicles sprang up, and Parliament was prevailed upon to impose upon steam carriages heavy highway tolls that were in effect prohibitory. Sir Charles Dance suspended his operations. Gurney petitioned the House of Commons for relief. Several committees in 1831, 1834 and 1835 investigated the subject and reported strongly in favor of steam carriages, but no legislation could be secured, and Gurney was forced to give up further introduction of steam carriages.

He continued his experimenting in other directions, invented the stove that bore his name, introduced new methods of lighting and ventilating the Houses of Parliament, and was otherwise active in scientific pursuits. He was a magistrate for Cornwall and Devonshire, and in 1863 was knighted in recognition of his discoveries and inventions.

By writers of that period Gurney received a great deal of credit and an abundance of advertising for his work. He was especially conspicuous in the Parliamentary investigations regarding steam carriages. On the whole, however, it is generally considered that he was proclaimed far beyond his merits, especially in comparison with such rivals as Hancock, Maceroni and others.

THOMAS BLANCHARD

Born in Sutton, Mass., June 24, 1788. Died, April 16, 1864.

Blanchard received a common school education, and before he had entered his teens his mechanical genius began to show itself. At thirteen years of age he invented a machine for paring apples, and shortly after, a machine for making tacks. His great work was the invention of a machine for turning out articles of irregular form from wood and metals. His lathes for this purpose were put in operation by the United States Government in the armories at Harper's Ferry, Va., and Springfield, Mass.

Becoming interested in the subject of steam propulsion he made, in 1826, a steamboat that was successfully tried on the Connecticut River, running from Hartford, Conn., to Springfield, Mass. Afterward, he built a boat of larger size, that drew eighteen inches of water, and ran this up the Connecticut River, from Springfield, Mass., to Vermont. He also built other boats for use on the Alleghany River.

The subjects of railroads and locomotive power on land interested him for a short time, and in 1825, after he had completed his engagement with the United States armories, he built, at Springfield, Mass., a carriage driven by steam for use on the common road. This was the first real steam carriage constructed in this country, the Philadelphia machine of Evans being but a rude affair, although it involved the essential principles of steam propulsion. The Blanchard carriage was perfectly manageable, could turn corners and go backwards and forwards with all the readiness of a well-trained horse, and on ascending a hill the power could be increased. Its performance on the highway was altogether satisfactory, and a patent was issued to its inventor.

Blanchard endeavored to secure support to build a railroad in Massachusetts, and the joint committee on roads and canals of the Massachusetts Legislature, in January, 1826, endorsed the model of his railway and steam carriage, and recommended them "to all the friends of internal improvements." Notwithstanding this report, capitalists viewed the project as visionary, and Blanchard met with no greater success when he subsequently applied to the Legislature of New York. Giving up his plans he thenceforward devoted his attention to the subject of steam navigation.

Blanchard was a prolific inventor, having taken out no less than thirty or forty patents for as many different inventions. He did not reap great benefit from his labors, for many of his inventions scarcely paid the cost of getting them up, while others were appropriated without payment to him, or even giving him credit. His machine for turning irregular forms was his most notable work, and even of that, others sought to defraud him. To defend himself he was forced to go to the courts and even to Congress, before he succeeded in establishing his rights. After the success of this machine he made other improvements in the manufacture of arms, constructing thirteen different machines that were operated in the government armories.

JOHNSON

Two brothers Johnson had a small engineering establishment in Philadelphia, in 1828. They put upon the streets in that year a vehicle that J. G. Pangborn, in his The World's Rail Way, says was "the first steam wagon built, and actually operated as such, in the United States." The same writer, describing this wagon, says that it had a single cylinder set horizontally, with a connecting-rod attachment with a single crank at the middle of the driving-axle. Its two driving-wheels were eight feet in diameter and made of wood, the same as those on an ordinary road wagon. The two forward or guiding wheels were much smaller than the others, and were arranged in the usual manner of a common wagon. It had an upright boiler hung up behind, shaped like a huge bottle, the smoke-stack coming out through the center of the top. The safety-valve was held down by a weight and lever, and the horses in the neighborhood did not take at all kindly to the puffing of the machine as it jolted over the rough streets. Generally it ran well, and could take without difficulty reasonable grades in the streets and roadways. During its existence, however, it knocked down a number of awning-posts, ran into and broke several window fronts, and sometimes was altogether unmanageable. Like all others of their day, however, the Johnsons were ahead of their time. There was no demand for their steam wagon, road conditions made it unavailable and the machine itself was, despite much merit, really not much more than a suggestion of better things three-quarters of a century later.

Walter Hancock

Born in Marlborough, Wiltshire, England, June 16, 1799. Died May 14, 1852.

The father of Walter Hancock was James Hancock, a timber merchant and cabinet maker. Walter received a common school education, and then was apprenticed to a watchmaker and jeweler in London. The bent of his inclination, however, was toward engineering, and he turned his attention to experimenting along the lines that were at that time absorbing the thoughts and efforts of those men of England interested in mechanical and scientific subjects.

He was foremost among those who in the early part of the nineteenth century were engaged in trying to solve the problem of steam carriage locomotion on the common highways. The story of his work in this direction is fully told by himself in his Narrative of Twelve Years' Experiments, 1824-36, Demonstrative of the Practicability and Advantage of Employing Steam Carriages on Common Roads, a book published in London, in 1838. This volume contains a full account of his labors, and descriptions of all the carriages that he built and ran. The following extract from the introduction of the book shows in what esteem Hancock regarded himself and what estimate he placed upon the value of his work:

"The author of these pages believes he should offend alike against truth and genuine modesty were he to yield to any of the steam carriage inventors who have appeared in his day, in a single particular of desert; he began earlier (with one abortive exception) and has persevered longer and more unceasingly than any of them. He was the first to run a steam carriage for hire on a common road, and is still the only person who has ventured in a steam vehicle to traverse the most crowded streets of the metropolis at the busiest periods of the day; he has built a greater number of steam carriages (if not better) than anyone else, and has been thus enabled to try a greater variety of forms of construction, out of which to choose the best."

In 1824, Hancock invented a steam engine in which the ordinary cylinder and piston were replaced by two flexible steam receivers, composed of several layers of canvas firmly united together by coatings of dissolved caoutchouc, or india-rubber, and thus enabled to resist a pressure of steam of sixty pounds upon the square inch. This engine he tried to adapt to steam carriages, but found that he could not get the requisite degree of power for locomotion, although it worked very well as a stationary engine of four horse-power at his factory in Stratford. Next he invented a tubular boiler with sixteen horizontal tubes, each connected with each other by lesser tubes, so that the water or steam might circulate through the entire series. This boiler was subsequently changed by arranging the tubes vertically, and a patent was taken out in 1825.

After further experiments and improvements, Hancock finally made a vehicle to travel on three wheels, getting power from a pair of vibrating or trunnion engines fixed upon the crank-axle of the fore wheels. Experimental trips of this carriage were made from the Stratford shop to Epping Forest,

Paddington, Hounslow, Croydon, Fulham, and elsewhere. Some changes were made in the vehicle, and finally the trunnion engines were put aside and fixed ones substituted.

This improved carriage, the first in a long series built by Hancock, was named the Infant. The body was in the form of a double-body coach, or omnibus, with seats for passengers inside and out. The bulk of the machinery was placed in the rear of the carriage, a boiler and a fire being beneath it. Between the boiler and the passengers' seats was the engine and a place for the engineer. A pair of inverted fixed engines working vertically on a crank-shaft furnished the power. The steering apparatus was in front. The whole carriage was on one frame supported by four springs on the axle of each wheel. The carriage was capable of carrying sixteen passengers besides the engineer and guide. Its total weight, including coke and water, but exclusive of attendants and passengers, was about three and one-half tons. The wheel tires were three and one-half inches wide, and the diameter of the hind wheels four feet.

In February, 1831, the Infant began to run on regular trips between Stratford and London. In 1832 a second carriage, similar to the Infant, was built, and called the Era. It was constructed for the London and Brighton Steam Carriage Company, to ply between London and Greenwich. The following year a third carriage, the Enterprise, was completed, for the London and Paddington Steam Car Company, and was run between London and Paddington.

Hancock took the Infant on a long trip from Stratford to London and Brighton, in October, 1832.

Eleven passengers were carried, and the carriage kept a speed of nine miles an hour on the level, and six to eight miles an hour up grade. On the return one mile up hill was made at the rate of seventeen miles an hour. Another trip to Brighton was made in September of the next year at an average speed of twelve miles an hour actual traveling. At Brighton the new carriage attracted much attention, and was exhibited for several days on trips in and around the town. After the Enterprise, the Autopsy came from the Hancock shops, in September, 1833. This carriage was run on trial about Brighton and in London streets, and for about a month was run for hire between Finsbury Square and Pentonville.

A small steam drag or tug to draw an attached coach or omnibus was the next production of the Hancock establishment, which had already attained more than local fame. This was built for a Herr Voigtlander, of Vienna, and on one of its trial trips it carried ten persons and an attached four-wheeled carriage with six persons in it. With this load a speed of fourteen miles an hour on the level was attained, and eight to nine miles an hour on up grades.

Beginning in August, 1834, the Era and the Autopsy were run daily in London between the City, Moorgate and Paddington. During the ensuing four months over four thousand passengers were carried. Each coach carried from ten to twelve passengers, and the trip from Moorgate to Paddington, five miles, was made in a half hour, including stops. On the trial trip a speed of twelve miles an hour, exclusive of stops, was maintained.

Later in the same year the Era, with its name changed to the Erin, was sent to Dublin, Ireland, where it was exhibited and run in and about the city, by Hancock, for eight days, before it was reshipped to Stratford. Next in turn came a drag of larger size than any before built, with an engine of greater capacity. On the trial trip this drew, on a level road, at a speed of ten miles an hour, three omnibuses and one stage coach with fifty passengers. In July, 1835, the trip to Reading, a distance of thirty-eight miles, was made in three hours forty minutes twenty-five seconds; actual running time, exclusive of stops, three hours eight minutes ten seconds, at a moving rate of over twelve miles an hour. Subsequently, this drag was made over into a carriage, like the others of the Hancock type, fitted for eighteen passengers, and named the Automaton.

In August, 1835, the Erin ran from London to Marlborough, a distance of seventy-eight miles, in seven hours forty-nine minutes, exclusive of stops, averaging nine and six-tenths miles an hour. The return from Marlborough to London was accomplished in seven hours thirty-six minutes, exclusive of stops, an average of nine and eight-tenths miles an hour. In the same month the Erin made the run from London to Birmingham at the rate of ten miles an hour.

In 1836, Hancock ran all his carriages on a regular route on the Stratford and Islington roads for a period of twenty weeks, making in that time seven hundred and twelve trips, covering four thousand two hundred miles, and carrying twelve thousand seven hundred and sixty-one passengers.

After running his carriages for several years dissensions in the companies that were promoting the new means of travel, and the increasing efficiency of railways, led to the discontinuance of Hancock's energy in this direction. Thereafter he built only a steam phaeton for his personal use; this had seats for three, and was used about the City, Hyde Park and the London suburbs. Hancock's steam vehicles were ten in number—the experimental three-wheeler, the trunnion-engine Infant, the fixed engine Infant, the Era, afterward the Erin, the Enterprise, the Autopsy, the Austrian drag, the Irish drag, the Automaton, and the phaeton.

Hancock turned his attention in the later years of his life to developing the use of india-rubber, in connection with his brother, Thomas Hancock, who was one of the foremost rubber manufacturers of England. He secured several patents for improvements in manufacturing rubber.

At the time when Hancock was at work upon his steam carriages, Gurney was also in the front and there was considerable jealousy between the two. Dr. Lardner and others were active in exploiting Gurney, while Hancock was supported in controversies by Alexander Gordon, Luke Hebert and others. That Hancock achieved most in the way of definite results and that his experimenting and accomplishments were more markedly along thoroughly intelligent and conservatively practical mechanical lines than any of his rivals is now generally conceded. His carriages were admirable productions as road vehicles, well-built, attractive and comfortable.

William T. James

An engineer of New York, who was engaged in experimenting about 1829 James made, in his shop in Eldridge Court, several small models of vehicles that proved sufficiently satisfactory. His first engine had two-inch cylinders and four-inch stroke. This ran around a track on the floor of his shop, and drew a train of four cars, carrying an apprentice boy on each car. James' second locomotive was mounted on three wheels, two drivers in the rear and a steering wheel, and it ran on the floor or sidewalk.

In 1829, James, satisfied with his experimenting, built a steam carriage capable of carrying passengers, and with this he made very good time over the streets and roadways in and about the metropolis. He then adopted the rotary cylinders instead of the reciprocating, in his engine, which had two six-inch cylinders, and was supported on three wheels. On each cylinder were two fixed eccentrics, one for the forward and one for the backing motion. The slide valve of one cylinder had a half-inch lap at each end, and exhausted its steam into the other.

In 1830, James made his fourth full-size steam carriage. This was a three-wheeled vehicle, the rear wheels being drivers three feet in diameter, and the third the front or steering wheel. In 1831, in a competition for the best locomotive engine adapted to the Baltimore and Ohio Railroad Company, James built his fifth locomotive, and the first one to run on rails. His engine did not secure the prize, but the company, thinking his machine contained valuable ideas, entered into an arrangement with him for further experimenting.

Francis Maceroni

Born in Manchester, England, in 1788. Died in London, July 25, 1846.

The father of Francis Maceroni was Peter Augustus Maceroni who, with two brothers, served in a French regiment in the American Revolution. After that conflict was ended he went to England and settled in Manchester, where he was Italian agent for British manufacturers.

Francis Maceroni was educated in the Roman Catholic school, in Hampshire; at the Dominican Academy, in Surrey, and at the college at Old Hall Green, near Puckerbridge, Hertfordshire. During a period of ten years, from 1803 to 1813, he lived in Rome and Naples as a young gentleman of elegant leisure. In 1813 he began the study of anatomy and medicine, but had not gone far in those pursuits before his vagrom disposition took him in another direction. He became aide-de-camp to Murat, King of Naples, with the rank of Colonel of Cavalry. His service with Murat took him on missions to England and France, and for a time he was a prisoner of the French authorities.

After two years of this military service, he returned to England, and retained his residence there for the rest of his life. He did not remain at home long, however, for he was with Sir George MacGregor at Porto Bello, in 1819; became a brigadier-general of the new republic of Colombia, and in 1821 saw service in Spain with General Pepe.

Returning again to England, he came before the public as an advocate of a ship canal across the Isthmus, between the Atlantic and Pacific oceans, and also promoted a company, called The Atlantic and Pacific Junction and South American Mining and Trading Company, with a capital of one million pounds sterling. The company collapsed in the commercial panic of 1825, and this soldier of fortune in 1829 went to Constantinople to assist the Turks against the Russians. In London again in 1831, Maceroni was engaged for the rest of his life in the cause of highway steam locomotion, in which he accomplished a great deal.

Maceroni was second only to Walter Hancock as an inventor and builder of steam road carriages and as a promoter of travel by those vehicles. From 1825 to 1828 he was with Goldsworthy Gurney in London, but his real activity did not begin until 1831, when he became associated with John Squire. In 1833, Maceroni and Squire took out a patent for a multi-tubular boiler, which they applied to a steam carriage that one writer of that day described as "a fine specimen of indomitable perseverance." It often traveled at the rate of from eighteen to twenty miles an hour. The engines were placed horizontally underneath the carriage body, the boiler was arranged at the back, and a fan was used to urge the combustion of the fuel, the supply of which was regulated by the engineman, who had a seat behind. The passengers were placed in the open carriage body, and their seats were upon the tops of the water tanks. There were two cylinders seven and one-half inches in diameter, the stroke being fifteen and three-quarter inches. The diameter of the steam pipe was two and one-quarter inches, and that of the exhaust pipe was two and three-quarter inches.

The carriage attracted a great deal of attention, and much was written about it in the newspapers of the time. Once the trip was taken to Harrow-on-the-Hill, a distance of nine miles, in fifty-eight minutes, without the full power of steam being on at any time. For several weeks in the early part of 1834 the carriage was running daily from Oxford Street to Edgeware. Several trips were made to Uxbridge, when the roads were in very bad condition, but the journey from the Regent's Circus, Oxford Street, a distance of sixteen miles, was often performed in a little over an hour. A trip to Watford was made, and one of the passengers thus described the experience from Bushby Heath into the village of Watford:

"We set off from the starting place amid the cheers of the villagers. The motion was so steady that we could have read with ease, and the noise was no worse than that produced by a common vehicle. On arriving at the summit of Clay Hill, the local and inexperienced attendant neglected to clog the wheel until it became impossible. We went thundering down the hill at the rate of thirty miles an hour. Mr. Squire was steersman, and never lost his presence of mind. It may be conceived what amazement a thing of this kind, flashing through the village of Bushy, occasioned among the inhabitants. The people seemed petrified on seeing a carriage without horses. In the busy and populous town of Watford the sensation was similar—the men gazed in speechless wonder; the women clapped their hands. We turned round at the end of the street in magnificent style, and ascended Clay Hill at the same rate as the stage coaches drawn by five horses."

Maceroni made two steam carriages, but in 1834 he separated from Squire, and becoming short of funds fell into the clutches of Asda, an Italian Jew, who persuaded him to let the two carriages go to the Continent. One was sent to Brussels, where it ran successfully, and the other went to Paris. The performance of the latter was thus described in the columns of a Paris journal: "The steam carriage brought to perfection in England by Colonel Maceroni, ran along the Boulevards as far as the Rue Faubourg du Temple. It turned with the greatest facility, ran the whole length of the Boulevards back again, and along the Rue Royale, to the Place Louis XV. This carriage is very elegant, much lighter, and by no means so noisy as the one we saw here some months ago, and it excited along its way the surprise and applause of the astonished spectators. All the hills on the paved Boulevard were ascended with astonishing rapidity. One of our colleagues was in this carriage the whole of its running above described, and he declares that there is not the least heat felt inside from the fire, and that conversation can be kept up so as to be heard at a much lower tone than in most ordinary carriages."

Asda sold the carriage and the patent for a large sum of money, and swindled Maceroni out of all his share. For years the inventor was in the direst extremes of poverty. In 1841 he succeeded in securing the support of The General Steam Carriage Company to construct and run carriages under his patent. Disagreement between the directors and the manufacturing engineer again brought to Maceroni disaster, from which he was never able to recover.

RICHARD ROBERTS

Born in 1789. Died in March, 1864.

Roberts was best known as a Manchester, England, engineer, of the firm of Sharp, Roberts & Co. He built a steam road locomotive that was first tried in December, 1833. Three months later the machine was subjected to a second trial. The carriage went out under the guidance of Mr. Roberts, with forty passengers. It proceeded about a mile and a half, made a difficult turn where the road was narrow, and returned to the works without accident. The maximum speed on the level was nearly twenty miles an hour. Hills were mounted easily. No doubt existed of the engine being speedily put in complete and effective condition for actual service. During another experimental trip in April of the same year, the locomotive met with an accident caused by some of the boiler tubes giving way, allowing the steam to escape and the fuel to be scattered about. No one was seriously injured, and none of the passengers was hurt.

Roberts invented the compensating gear that he first used on his steam carriage. This gear superseded claw clutches, friction bands, ratchet-wheels, and other arrangements for obtaining the full power of both the driving-wheels, and at the same time allowing for the engine to turn the sharpest corner. In 1839, Roberts invented an arrangement for communicating power to both driving-wheels at all times, whether turning to the right or left. During the latter years of his life this famous engineer lived in exceedingly straitened circumstances, and he died in poverty.

JOHN SCOTT RUSSELL

Born at Parkhead, near Glasgow, Scotland, May 8, 1808. Died June 8, 1882, at Ventnor.

The father of John Scott Russell was David Russell, a Scottish clergyman, and the son was originally intended for the church. His mind was more inclined toward mechanics than theology, and he entered a workshop in order to learn the trade of engineering. Studying at the Universities of Edinburgh, St. Andrews and Glasgow, he was graduated from Glasgow when he was sixteen years of age. In 1832, upon the death of Sir John Leslie, Professor of Natural Philosophy at Edinburgh University, Russell was elected to fill the vacancy temporarily. Shortly after that he began his celebrated investigations into the nature of the sea waves, as a preliminary study to improving the forms of ships. As a result of these researches he developed the wave-line system for the construction of vessels. In 1837 he received a gold medal of the Royal Society of Engineers, and was elected a member of the Council of that Society for a paper that he read "on the laws by which water opposes resistance to the motion of floating bodies." At that time he was manager of the shipbuilding words at Greenock, and under his supervision and according to his designs several ships were built with lines based on his wave system. Among these were four of the new fleet of the West India Mail Company.

Russell removed to London in 1844, and became a Fellow of the Royal Society in 1847. He was vice-president of the Institute of Civil Engineers and secretary of the Society of Arts. For many years he was a shipbuilder on the Thames, and supervised the construction of the celebrated steamship Great Eastern. He was one of the promoters and vice-president of the Institute of Naval Architects, and a pioneer in advocating the construction of iron-clad men-of-war. He published many papers, principally upon naval architecture.

It was while he was residing in Edinburgh that he took out a patent for a steam locomotive to be used on the common roads. The boiler that he invented was multi-tubular, with the furnace and the return tubes on the same level, and similar to a marine boiler. The boiler everywhere consisted of opposite and parallel surfaces, and these surfaces were connected by stays of small diameter. The copper plates of the boiler were only one-tenth of an inch thick. When put to actual test the weakness of the boiler thus constructed was fully demonstrated.

The engine had two vertical cylinders, twelve inches in diameter and with twelve inches stroke. The engine was mounted upon laminated springs, arranged so that each spring in its flexure described, at a particular point, such a circle as was also described by the main axle in its motion round the crank shaft. This arrangement was intended to correct any irregularities in the road so that they would not interfere with the proper working of the spur gearing. Exhaust steam was turned into the chimney to create a blast. Water and coke were carried on a separate tender on two wheels, coupled to the rear of the engine. Spare tenders, filled, were kept in readiness at different stations on the road.

These tenders, mounted upon springs, had seats back and front for passengers. To work the locomotive three persons were required, a steersman on the front seat, an engineer on the back seat outside above the engines, and a fireman stationed on the footplate in front of the boiler.

On the order of the Steam Carriage Company, of Scotland, six of these coaches were built by the Grove House Engine Works, of Edinburgh. They were substantially constructed and very elaborately fitted up. As was said at the time, they were "in the style and with all the comfort and elegance of the most costly gentleman's carriage." They ran very successfully for some time, during 1834, between St. George's Square, Glasgow, and Paisley. There was a service of six coaches once an hour. Each carriage accommodated six passengers inside and twenty outside, and sometimes drew, in addition, a dogcart laden with six passengers, and the necessary fuel and water. These dogcarts were used as relays on the road, being kept ready constantly. Public opposition to these coaches developed here as it had done in London about the same period. Road trustees objected to them on the ground that they wore out the roads too rapidly. Obstructions of stones, logs of wood, and other things were placed in their way, but the coaches generally went on in spite of these. Ordinary horse-drawn road carriages were more damaged and hindered than the Russell coaches, and even heavy carts were compelled to abandon travel on the obstructed roads and take roundabout courses, greatly to the discomfiture of the drivers.

One day, however, a heavy strain, unusually severe, caused by jolting over the rough road, broke a wheel, and the weight of the coach falling on the boiler caused an explosion. Five persons were killed, and as a result of this accident the Court of Session interdicted the further travel of these carriages in Scotland. The Steam Carriage Company brought an action for damages against the trustees of the turnpike road for having compelled them to withdraw the carriages from the Glasgow and Paisley road by "wantonly, wrongfully and maliciously accumulating masses of metal, stones and rubbish on the said road, in order to create such annoyance and obstruction as might impede, overturn, or destroy the steam coaches belonging to the plaintiffs," but nothing seems to have come of this action.

No longer used in Scotland, two of Russell's coaches were sent to London. There they were engaged in running with passengers between London and Greenwich, or Kew Bridge. Several trips were made to Windsor. After about a year they were offered for sale, and, on exhibition preparatory to sale, they started every day from Hyde Park Corner to make a journey to Hammersmith. But they remained unsold, and were shortly forgotten.

Had conditions been more encouraging Russell might have achieved as great success in his land as in his water vehicles. He was a man of rare scientific attainments, and his work in ship designing and building put him in the front rank of naval architects and builders of his day. In addition to his work, already mentioned, he built a big steamer to transport railway trains across Lake Constance.

W. H. Church

A physician of Birmingham, England, Dr. W. H. Church gave many years to the study of steam locomotion. Several patents were secured by him between 1832 and 1835, and in the latter year a common road carriage, built according to his plans, was brought out.

The Church vehicle had a framework of united iron plates or bars, bolted on each side of the woodwork to obtain strength. Well trussed and braced, this framework enclosed a space between a hind and fore body of the carriage, and of the same height as the latter, and contained the engine, boiler, and other machinery. The boiler consisted of a series of vertical tubes, placed side by side, through each of which a pipe passed, and was secured at the bottom of the boiler tube; the interior pipe constituted the flue, which first passed in through a boiler tube, and was then bent like a syphon, and passed down another until it reached as low or lower than the bottom of the fireplace, whence it passed off into a general flue in communication with an exhausting apparatus. Two fans were employed, one to blow in air, and the other to draw it out; they were worked by straps from the crank shaft. The wheels of the carriage were constructed with the view to rendering them elastic, to a certain degree, in two different ways: First, the felloes were made of several successive layers of broad wooden hoops, covered with a thin iron tire, having lateral straps to bind the hoops together; second, these binding straps were connected by hinge joints to a kind of flat steel springs, somewhat curved, which formed the spokes of the wheels.

These spring spokes were intended to obviate the necessity, in a great measure, of the ordinary springs, and the elasticity of the periphery was designed so that the yielding of the circle should prevent the wheel from turning without propelling.

Church also proposed, in addition to spring felloes, spring spokes, and the ordinary springs, to employ air springs, and for that purpose provided two or more cylinders, made fast to the body of the carriage, in a vertical position, closed at top, and furnished with a piston, with packing similar to the cap-leather packing of the hydraulic press. This piston was kept covered with oil, to preserve it in good order, and a piston rod connected it with the supporting frame of the carriage. Motion was communicated by two oscillating steam cylinders suspended on the steam and exhaust pipes over the crank shaft. The crank shaft and driving-wheel axle were connected by means of chains passing about pitched pulleys.

To introduce the Church coach, the London and Birmingham Steam Carriage Company was organized. The first carriage built for the company was an imposing vehicle, something like a big circus van, elaborately ornamented and with a large spheroidal wheel in front. It carried about forty passengers on top, in omnibus fashion, and the driver sat on a raised seat near the roof. A fair rate of speed was maintained, fifteen miles on the level, but the boiler was damaged, and horses hauled the engine back to the factory. Other carriages were subsequently brought out, but they all failed to meet the requirements of travel on the rough roads that existed at that time in England.

Jean Joseph Etienne Lenoir

Born at Mussy-la-Ville, Luxembourg, January 12, 1822. Died, July, 1900, at La Varnne Chemevieves, near Paris.

When Lenoir came to Paris in 1838 he had but an ordinary education and was without resources. For a time he served as a waiter in order to earn money to become an enameler and decorator. In 1847, he invented a new white enamel and four years after invented a galvano plastic process for raised work. Many other inventions were made by him, among them being an electric motor in 1856, a water meter in 1857, an automatic regulator for dynamos, the well-known gas motor that bears his name, and a system of autographic telegraphing.

It is claimed that in September, 1863, Lenoir put a gas engine of his non-compressor type, of one and a half horse-power, on wheels and made an experimental run to Joinville-le-Paris and back. The motor, running at one hundred revolutions, it is said, took them there in one and a half hours. He thereupon abandoned such trials, and tried his engines in a boat, and in 1865 put a six horse-power in one, but the insignificant speed possible with his engine caused him to abandon that also.

The Academy of Science of Paris decorated M. Lenoir and the Society of Encouragement gave him the grand prize of Argenteuil, amounting to twelve thousand francs. For his patriotic services at the siege of Paris, during the Franco-Prussian war, he was made a naturalized Frenchman. In 1880, he published in Paris a work treating of his researches into the tanning of leather.

AMEDÈE BOLLÈE

In April, 1873, Amedèe Bollèe, of Le Mans, France, the noted French engineer, filed a patent for a steam road vehicle and two years later he built the steam stage that he named Obeissante. Toward the end of that year this stage was run in and about Paris, where it created something of a sensation. It was even chronicled in the songs of the day and was made a topic of amusement at the variety theatres. This steam omnibus made twenty-eight kilometers in an hour. It is claimed to have been the first creation of the man to whose family much credit is due for the modern French automobile.

Between 1873 and 1875, Bollèe made several carriages. In 1876, he worked with Dalifol and made a tram-car that would carry fifty passengers. This vehicle was put into the steam omnibus service in Rouen. Two years later he made another steam omnibus that he called La Mancelle. This vehicle, in June of that year, was run from Paris to Vienna and developed a speed on level roads of twenty-two miles an hour. In Vienna this vehicle was the subject of much talk and was largely caricatured.

In 1880, Bollèe built another omnibus, La Nouvelle. This vehicle was entered in the Paris-Bordeaux competition in 1895, and was the only steam carriage that covered the course in that race. Bollèe has been a conspicuous exponent of the steam carriage in France from the time he commenced as far back as 1873. The vehicles that he has built were in many instances pioneers in their class, and have been exceedingly serviceable and successful. They have made the name of Bollèe notable.

George B. Selden

Born in the fifties, George B. Selden came of a family of jurists, whose ancestors were early Connecticut settlers. Among them were several eminent scientific men. His father, Henry Rogers Selden, was born in Lyme, Conn., October 14, 1805, and died in Rochester, N. Y., September 18, 1885; was Judge of the Supreme Court of the State of New York, and is still remembered by men of that generation as one of the most accomplished lawyers and jurists who occupied that bench in the last century.

George B. Selden attended Yale University, and while equipping himself for his legal career, following in the footsteps of his father, indulged his natural predilection for scientific work. While practicing law in Rochester, N. Y., he devoted much time to the problem of self-propelled vehicles on common roads, in which, as early as the sixties, he was then interested. The study of this art led to a very full analysis of the possibilities of different means of propulsion, with, as a result, the conclusion that the light, liquid hydro-carbon concussion engine must eventually fill the exacting requirements of road vehicles. His further experimenting that was carried on during the seventies, and the actual constructing, so convinced him in his deductions that the record is found in the United States Patent Office of his filing an application for patent in May, 1879, with a Patent Office model of his gasoline vehicle. For more details, reference must be made to his patent, No. 549160, subsequently issued in November, 1895. Thereafter in a general report treating of important and leading inventions in various fields this was referred to by the Commissioner of Patents as the pioneer patent in its class.

Of Selden's voluminous and persistent work and his many engines and models more detailed information cannot be here given. His fundamental patent at present is involved in extensive litigation, although it is recognized by manufacturers of gasoline vehicles who, to-day, are producing from eighty to ninety per cent of the output of the United States. Of his work along the lines of improvements in details of his main invention, the gasoline automobile *per se,* and kindred matters all of which have or will have a great bearing upon automobile construction and operation, it is not at this time possible to dwell at length.

Selden is known as an exceedingly able attorney in his specialty, while his active connection with the extensive reaper and binder litigation, in all of which he appeared prominently, established for him an enviable reputation. Those who have had the privilege of a closer personal acquaintance know of his great fund of scientific knowledge in various arts, as well as his most interesting accumulations of data as a result of his personal researches.

Selden is a patentee in other fields beside that of the gasoline automobile and his achievements have been numerous and of exceeding importance. He is also a chemist of more than ordinary ability and has applied himself as a close student to this line of scientific investigation. As a result he has made notable discoveries that, although not yet given to the world, will, it is confidently believed by those acquainted with them, prove to be of the greatest scientific value.

Siegfried Marcus

Marcus was an ingenious mechanic. In early life he made dental instruments and apparatus for a magician in Vienna. For his construction of a thermopile he received a prize and to his further credit as an inventor are placed an arc lamp, Rhumkoff coil carbureter, a high candle-power petroleum lamp, magneto-electro machines, a microphone and various other things in many branches of science.

It is claimed that about the middle seventies of the last century he carried on experiments with a gas engine that had a spring-connected piston rod. He mounted this vertically on an ordinary horse vehicle and connected it directly with a cranked rear axle, carrying two flywheels in place of the regular road wheels. He is said to have made trials of this vehicle at night in Vienna. If this was so he was apparently trying to keep his plan secret and succeeded very well. Aside from general references nothing of importance revealed itself concerning this vehicle and Marcus' experiments with it, until very recently when interest in the historic development of the automobile has stimulated anew investigation into the endeavors of the early inventors.

In 1882 the motor work of Marcus was principally preparatory to his new engine construction. It included experimenting with an Otto engine run with petroleum and a vaporizer and electric ignition with magneto. In 1883 he constructed a closed or two-cycled motor and thereafter had engines made in Budapest and elsewhere. One of these motors he put on wheels, but this was abandoned for other ideas that came from his fertile mind.

Carl Benz

Born, November 26, 1844, at Karlsruhe, Baden, Germany.

The early education of Carl Benz was acquired at the Lyceum until his seventeenth year and then at the Technical High School of his native city for four more years. This was followed by three years of practical work in the shops of the Karlsruhe Machine Works. When he was twenty-eight years of age, in 1872, after further experience in Mannheim, Pforzheim and Vienna, he opened workshops of his own in Mannheim.

In 1880 he began to commercialize a two-cycle stationary engine. In 1883 he organized his business as Benz & Co., and produced his first vehicle in 1884. In the beginning of 1885 his three-wheeled vehicle ran through the streets of Mannheim, Germany, attracting much attention with its noisy exhaust. This was the subject of his patent dated January 29, 1886, claimed by him to be the first German patent on a light oil motor vehicle. This embodied a horizontal flywheel belt transmission through a differential and two chains to the wheels; but it is noteworthy primarily as having embodied a four-cycle, water jacketed, three-quarter horsepower engine, with electric ignition.

In 1888, the Benz Company exhibited their vehicles at the Munich Exposition, where they attracted wide attention. This was followed by the exhibition at the Paris show in 1889, by the engineer Roger, of another vehicle made under license that Roger had acquired from Benz and constructed by Panhard and Levassor.

While in 1899 the firm was converted into a stock company of three million marks capital, and then employed three hundred men, Carl Benz remained the leading spirit of the concern, technically, while the commercial work came under the direction of Julius Ganz. The able co-operation of these two has established the world-famous automobile enterprise looked upon by many as the pioneer producing works of its kind in Germany. Of late years motor boats have also been made by them, but their automobiles and those of their affiliated companies or licensees in other countries still stand in the first rank.

GOTTLIEB DAIMLER

Born at Schorndorf, Wurtemburg, March 17, 1834. Died at Cannstadt, near Stuttgart, March 6, 1899.

After receiving a technical and scientific training at the Polytechnic School at Stuttgart, 1852-59, Daimler spent two years, 1861-63, as an engineer in the Karlsruhe Machine Works, becoming foreman there. In 1872 he entered the Gas Engine Works at Deutz, near Cologne, and became director of that establishment. Within ten years that shop, better known as the Otto Engine Works, grew from a small place into a large, well-organized and famous establishment. In 1882 he removed to Cannstadt to give his entire attention to the light-weight internal-combustion auto motor, with which his career was so completely identified, and the successful application of which earned for him the title, "the father of the automobile," in Germany, though that is, in fact, contested by those familiar with the work of Benz.

Instead of using the uncertain-acting flame with the inconvenient speed limitations, Daimler invented and introduced in 1883 the so-called hot-tube ignition. This consisted of a metal or porcelain tube attached to the compression space of the cylinder in such a manner that the interior of the tube was in continual communication with the compression space. A gas flame, continually burning under the tube, maintained it at a glowing red heat, so that the mixed charge of air and gas, when compressed into the tube, became fully and effectively ignited. Experience showed that by a proper regulation of the temperature of the hot tube the ignition could be made to take place at any desired point in the compression, and thus the complicated, slow and uncertain slide flame ignition was replaced by a simple device, without moving parts, altogether satisfactory and reliable. The especial feature of the hot-tube ignition, however, was soon found to be the increased speed which it permitted. By its use the rotative speed could be increased eight to ten times over the older motor, and hence the weight could be reduced in nearly the same proportion.

This fact at once showed Daimler that the application of the internal-combustion motor to mechanically propelled vehicles had become a possibility, and that, with the use of hydro-carbon vapor as fuel, and the high-speed hot-tube motor, the petroleum automobile might become a practical possibility. He therefore severed his connection with the Otto Engine Works at Deutz, and returning to Cannstadt, near Stuttgart, his early home, he devoted his entire time and attention to the design of a light petroleum motor and motor vehicle. The result was the production, in 1885, of a motor-bicycle, in which the motor was placed directly under the seat, between the legs of the rider. The petroleum was drawn from a tank, the supply being regulated by the valve. The motor was first set in motion by lighting a lamp and turning the crank a few times, the discharge passing through the chamber into an exhaust-pipe. After the motor had been fully started, the vehicle was set in motion by moving a lever, which drew a tightening pulley against the belt, and so caused the power to be transmitted from the shaft pulley to the wheel pulley. Changes of speed were attained by using pulleys of different sizes, similar to the cone pulleys on a lathe. This machine was put into successful action at Cannstadt on November 10, 1885.

An interesting feature in connection with the Daimler motor is the arrangement of the cooling-water circulation for the cylinder jacket. The water is contained in a tank, from which it is circulated in the cylinder jacket by means of a small rotary pump. From the jacket it passes to the cooler. This consists of a system of several hundred small tubes over which a blast of air is driven by a fan operated from the motor shaft. Since the speed of the fan increases with the speed of the motor, the cooling is proportional to the production of heat in the cylinder.

In addition to gas, which is applicable for stationary motors only, the fuel may be benzine of a specific gravity of sixty-eight or seventy one-hundredths, or ordinary lamp petroleum. The consumption varies according to the size of the motor, ranging from thirty-six to forty-five one-hundredths kilograms per horse-power hour for vehicles, or somewhat less for boats. He adapted these light motors to vehicles of many styles, and his persistent work in this connection has made the world-wide reputation of the Daimler Motoren Gesellschaft, now flourishing at Cannstadt, Germany.

In 1888-89 the French interest in the light motors led to their adoption by Panhard and Levassor. The type then developed and known as Phenix motors, were soon copied in part at least by many other French makers, resulting in a modified form there known as the Pygmée. Work at Cannstadt progressed steadily, however, and many pleasure vehicles were made as well as small boats.

The able assistance of William Maybach brought further credit to the company, particularly in view of the aspirating carbureter which, with such details as clutch and transmission mechanism, helped to perfect the Cannstadt automobiles. In the latter nineties the prominence of the Daimler Works as vehicle makers, distinguished from motor makers, again began to be noticed and soon their now famous Mercedes cars appeared. In recent years these machines have made remarkable records in races and all other branches of the sport. With a magnificent refinement of details in construction they are to-day looked upon as the pleasure vehicles *par excellence.*

They have had a large vogue in all parts of Europe and are accepted there as among the most satisfactory vehicles in their class that are now made. Many of them have been brought to the United States, where they have been and still are in great demand.

EVASSOR

Born at Marolles, in Hurepoix (Seine and Oise), January 21, 1843. Died, April 14, 1897.

Levassor was graduated from the Central School of Arts and Manufactures, Paris, in 1864. He was employed as an engineer at the Cockerill Works at Seriang, Belgium, and also with Durenne at Courbevoie, near Paris. In 1872 he entered the firm of Perrin & Panhard, the name of the concern being changed to Perrin, Panhard & Co. Upon the death of M. Perrin, he became the junior partner and the name of Panhard & Levassor was adopted. When Levassor died in 1897, the corporation of Panhard & Levassor was formed.

Levassor made many improvements in the machinery and output of Panhard & Levassor. Especially he perfected machines for wood-working and made important changes in the processes used for the cold cutting of hard metals. On the first appearance of gas motors he undertook their construction in France. It was in the establishment of Panhard & Levassor that the first motors were constructed under the system of Otto and Langen with atmospheric pressure, then the four-cycle engine of Otto and finally the two-cycle system of Benz and Ravell.

In 1886, when the Daimler petroleum motor appeared, he recognized the great part that it would play in practical application to the propulsion of vehicles and boats. He acquired the right to use it in France, and in 1887 exhibited, in Paris, a boat thus propelled. After several years he put forth the first automobile vehicle with motor in front.

LEON SERPOLLET

Serpollet is noted in France to-day as the champion of the steam automobile. In 1887, he appeared in Paris with his three-wheeler, two rear drive and one front steering wheel. With its light and safe generator his machine attracted much attention, but its use in the streets of the capital was temporarily prohibited, until the granting to him in 1891 of the first unrestricted license for such use resulted from his initiation of the prefect of police by driving that important personage in the steamer.

His generator, known as the "flash boiler," has been developed to a high state of perfection. The tubes of his boiler were heavy, flattened tubing, strengthened in that form by being transversally bent or grooved. He was helped doubtless to no small extent, in his work, by his association, about 1897, with a wealthy American, F. L. Gardner, who made possible the development of the large Gardner-Serpollet establishment in the Rue Stendhal, Paris.

While Serpollet has achieved a brilliant and well-deserved reputation in his native land, he is also recognized in other countries as one of the greatest living promoters of the steam branch of the automobile industry. His adherence to steam as the motive power in self-propelled road vehicles has been unremitting and energetic. Few men have done more than he to improve carriages in this class.

In 1900, Serpollet was made a Chevalier of the Legion of Honor. His sales to that date of five machines for the Shah of Persia and landaulets for the Maharajah of Mysore and other notables had given him much prominence at that time.

Louis and Marcel Renault

Born in Boulogne, France, the Renault Brothers, with general technical education, perseverance and ability, entered the field of automobile manufacturing only some six years ago, although they earlier gave to the subject much attention and study.

Having appreciated through personal experience the shortcomings of the gasoline tricycle, Louis Renault in October, 1898, manufactured, in his private shop, a small two-passenger vehicle, with a one and three-quarters horse-power motor, which eliminated the pedalling for starting, but was otherwise small and light as a tricycle. In January, 1899, he brought out a small four-wheeler with one and three-quarters horse-power motor in front, three speeds and chainless, or as now called propeller drive. The demand was immediate and large and resulted in the establishment of the works of Renault Frères, who began to make the first lot of these small vehicles in March of the same year. These won prizes in the Paris-Trouville, the Ostende and the Rambouillet runs, and one completed a three thousand six hundred kilometer tour through different parts of Europe and over the Alps.

The new model of 1900 had a three and one-half horse-power motor and thermo-syphon cooling system. Many honors were won with these, and notably that of Louis Renault's most successful use of one in the grand army maneuvers. But the output of three hundred and fifty showed the necessity for larger works. With the increased facilities of 1901, the product was doubled and the model increased to four and one-half horse-power, while eight and nine horse-power were winners in the Paris-Bordeaux and Paris-Berlin races.

In 1902 came another addition to the Billancourt works of Cloise to four thousand square meters area, and the Renault Brothers then changed their models to voiture légère, six to eight horse-power, steel tube frame and wood wheels—a full-fledged vehicle. They succeeded in the Circuit du Nord, organized by the Minister of Agriculture, for alcohol-motored vehicles. Then came the triumph of their twenty horse-power four-cylinder type in the great Paris-Vienna race, where it was pitted against forty and even seventy horse-power vehicles. The result was a great impetus commercially, and new shops accommodating a thousand workmen and covering thirteen thousand square meters, which produced one thousand four hundred vehicles in the following year.

Both brothers, who had always been at the wheel of their own cars in the years of racing, entered the memorable "race-of-death," Paris-Madrid, in May, 1903. Louis arrived first at Bordeaux, but his unfortunate brother Marcel, while close to victory, was killed with the overturning of his machine only a few kilometers from the goal. In memory of Marcel Renault a simple monument was unveiled at Billancourt May 26, 1904, on ground contributed by the municipal council; a bronze plate on one side of this perpetuates his triumphant entry into Vienna, showing his arrival at the finish.

Louis Renault, since continuing the business, has now produced larger machines, including the sixty to ninety horse-power made for the Vanderbilt race in America, October, 1904.

NOTED INVESTIGATORS

NOTED INVESTIGATORS

Simon Stevin,
Thomas Wildgosse,
David Ramsey,
Johann Hautsch,
Christiaan Huygens,
Stephen Farfleur,
Fernando Verbiest,
Isaac Newton,
Vegelius,
Elié Richard,
Gottfried Wilhelm von Leibnitz,
Humphrey Mackworth,
Denis Papin,
Vaucauson,
Robinson,
Erasmus Darwin,
Richard Lovell Edgeworth,
Francis Moore,
Planta,
J. S. Kestler,
Blanchard,
Thomas Charles Auguste Dallery,
James Watt,
Robert Fourness,
George Medhurst,
Andrew Vivian,

Du Quet,
J. H. Genevois,
John Dumbell,
William Brunton,
Thomas Tindall,
John Baynes,
Julius Griffiths,
Edmund Cartwright,
T. Burtsall,
T. W. Parker,
George Pocock,
Samuel Brown,
James Neville,
T. S. Holland,
James Nasmyth,
F. Andrews,
Harland,
Pecqueur,
James Viney,
Chevalier Bordino,
Clive,
Summers and Ogle,
Gibbs,
Charles Dance,
Joshua Field,
Dietz,
Yates,
G. Millichap,
James Caleb Anderson,
Robert Davidson,
W. G. Heaton,

F. Hill,
Goodman,
Norrgber,
J. K. Fisher,
R. W. Thompson,
Anthony Bernhard,
Battin,
Richard Dudgeon,
Lough and Messenger,
Thomas Rickett,
Daniel Adamson,
Stirling,
W. O. Carrett,
Richard Tangye,
T. W. Cowan,
Charles T. Hayball,
Isaac W. Boulton,
Armstrong,
Pierre Ravel,
L. T. Pyott,
A. Richter,
Raffard,
Charles Jeanteaud,
Sylvester Haywood Roper,
Copeland,
G. Bouton,
Count A. De Dion,
Armand Peugeot,
Radcliffe Ward,
Mors,
Magnus Volk,

BUTLER,
LE BLANT,
EMILE DELAHAYE,
ROGER,
GEORGES RICHARD,
POCHAIN,
LOUIS KRIEGER,
DE DETRICH,
DAVID SALOMONS,
LEON BOLLÈE,
JOSEPH GUEDON,
RENE DE KNYFF,
ADOLF CLEMENT,
A. DARRACQ,
JAMES GORDON BENNETT.

SIMON STEVIN

Born in Bruges, Holland, in 1548. Died in 1620.

Stevin was a noted mathematician, and also experimented in the construction of wheel vehicles about 1600. He built in his workshop at The Hague a wheeled vehicle that was propelled by sails. This was simply a tray or boat of wood, which hung close to the ground. It was borne on four wooden wheels, each one of which was five feet in diameter, and the after-axle was pivoted to form a rudder. A tall mast was carried amidships, and there was a small foremast that was stayed aft. Large square sails were carried on these masts. A trial trip of this sailing ship on land was made in 1600, when the journey from Scheveningen to Petten, a distance of forty-two miles, was made in about two hours. On this occasion some twenty-two passengers were carried. Prince Maurice of Holland steered, and among the passengers were Grotius, and the Spanish Admiral, Mendoza, who was then a prisoner of war in Holland.

Stevin also built a smaller sail vehicle, similar to the one just described, that carried from five to eight persons. Both carriages were used a great deal, running many miles on the Dutch coast. The smaller one was to be seen at Scheveningen as late as 1802. Grotius wrote a poem on these carriages. Bishop Wilkens, in England, also wrote about them in 1648, and showed a drawing that was made from a description given to him by those who had seen the car at work. Howell, a writer of the period, thus quaintly described the Stevin carriage: "This engine, that hath wheels and sails, will hold above twenty people, and goes with the wind, being drawn or moved by nothing else, and will run, the wind being good and the sails hois'd up, about fifteen miles an hour upon the even hard sands."

Thomas Wildgosse

In 1618, Thomas Wildgosse got out a patent for "newe, apte, or compendious formes or kinds of engines or instruments to ploughe grounds without horse or oxen; and to make boates for the carryage of burthens and passengers runn upon the water as swifte in calmes, and more safe in stormes, than boats full sayled in great wynnes." It is agreed by the best authorities that these vehicles were set in motion by gear worked by the hand of a driver, although Fletcher thinks that steam engines were intended. Additional patents were granted to Wildgosse in 1625.

David Ramsey

Associated with Thomas Wildgosse in his experimenting and patenting, in 1618, was David Ramsey, who at that time was Page of the Bed Chamber to James I. of England, and afterwards was Groom of the Privy Chamber to the same monarch. In 1644, Ramsey was again a partner in the grant of a patent for "a farre more easie and better waye for soweing of corne and grayne, and alsoe for the carrying of coaches, carts, drayes, and other things goeing on wheels, than ever yet was used and discovered." This may have been a manually or a steam propelled vehicle. It is most reasonable to suppose that it was the former.

Johann Hautsch

Born in 1595. Died in 1670.

Hautsch was a noted mathematician, and, experimenting in the construction of road vehicles, he built a mechanical carriage for use on common roads. This carriage was successfully run in Nuremberg, Germany, in 1649, and thereafter attracted a great deal of attention. It was propelled by a train of gears that turned the axle, being operated by two men who, secreted in the interior of the body, worked cranks. The finish of the body of this coach was very elaborate, being heavily carved and having fashioned in front the figure of a dragon, arranged to roll its eyes and spout steam and water, in order to terrify the populace and clear the way. On each side of the body were carved angels holding trumpets, which were constantly blown, the precursors, perhaps, of the automobile horns of to-day. The Hautsch coach was said to have gone as rapidly as one thousand paces an hour. One of the carriages which he built was sold to the Crown Prince of Sweden, and another to the King of Denmark. Not much more is known of the Hautsch vehicles, but it is a matter of record that the inventor was preceded by one whose name is unknown, but who ran a coach, mechanically propelled somewhat like this car, in January, 1447, near Nuremberg.

Christiaan Huygens

Born at The Hague, Holland, April 14, 1629. Died at The Hague, June 8, 1695.

Huygens received a good education, and at early age showed a singular aptitude for mathematics.

Soon after he was sixteen years of age he prepared papers on mathematical subjects that gave him pre-eminent distinction. He became noted as a physicist, astronomer and mathematician. He devoted some time to the consideration of improvements in road vehicular travel.

STEPHEN FARFLUER

Born in 1663.

Farfluer was a contemporary of Johann Hautsch, and was a skillful mechanician of Altderfanar, Nuremberg, Germany. About 1650 he made a dirigible vehicle propelled by man power, but as distinguished from that of his rival, Hautsch, this was a small carriage, being calculated only for one person. Being crippled, Farfluer used the wagon as his only means of getting about alone. It had hand cranks that drove the single front wheel by gears.

FERNANDO VERBIEST

Born near Courtrai, Belgium, 1623. Died in China in 1688.

Verbiest became a Jesuit missionary, and was a man of marked ability. After going to China he acquired a thorough knowledge of the language of that country, where he spent the greater part of his life. Under his Chinese name he wrote scientific and theological works in Chinese. He was appointed astronomer at the Pekin observatory, undertook the reformation of the Chinese calendar, superintended the cannon foundries, and was a great favorite of the Emperor.

About 1655 he made a small model of a steam carriage. This is described in the English edition of Huc's Christianity in China, in Muirhead's Life of James Watt, and in the Astronomia Europia, a work that is attributed to Verbiest, but was probably compiled from his works by another Jesuit priest and was published in Europe in 1689. The Verbiest model was for a four-wheeled carriage, on which an aeolipile was mounted with a pan of burning coals beneath it. A jet of steam from the aeolipile impinged upon the vanes of a wheel on a vertical axle, the lower end of the spindle being geared to the front axle. An additional wheel, larger than the supporting wheels, was mounted on an adjustable arm in a manner to adapt the vehicle to moving in a circular path. Another orifice in the aeolipile was fitted with a reed, so that the steam going through it imitated the song of a bird.

Isaac Newton

Born at Woolsthorpe, Lincolnshire, England, December 25, 1642. Died at Kensington, March 20, 1727.

Isaac Newton, who became one of the greatest mathematicians that the world ever knew, was the son of a farmer. He was educated at Trinity College, Cambridge, and in his early youth he mastered the principles of mathematics, as then known, and began original investigations to discover new methods. His great achievement was the discovery of the law of universal gravitation, but his genius was active in other directions, as the investigation of the nature of light, the construction of improved telescopes, and so on. He was a Member of Parliament in 1689 and 1701, and master of the mint, a lucrative position, from 1696 until the time of his death. In 1671 he was elected a member of the Royal Society, and was annually chosen to be its president, from 1703 until his death.

Newton was one of the first Englishmen to conceive the idea of the propulsion of vehicles by the power of steam. Taking up for consideration Hero's hollow ball filled with water from which steam was generated by the outward application of heat, he added these conclusions: "We have a more sensible effect of the elasticity of vapors if the hole be made bigger and stopped, and then the ball be laid upon the fire till the water boils violently; after this, if the ball be set upon little wheels, so as to move easily upon a horizontal plane, and the hole be opened, the vapors will rush out violently one way, and the wheels and the ball at the same time will be carried the contrary way." Beyond this philosophical suggestion, however, Newton never went. The steam carriage attributed to him by some writers is merely an imaginative creation, by writer or artist, based upon the above proposition.

Vegelius

A professor at Jena, Saxony, in the seventeenth century, Vegelius constructed, in 1679, a mechanical horse, which was propelled by springs and cased in the skin of a real horse. This machine is said to have traveled four German miles an hour.

Elié Richard

Born on the Island of Ré in 1645.

A physician of La Rochelle, France, Elié Richard was a man of science, and a considerable celebrity in his day. He had built, in 1690, a dirigible vehicle that he used to travel about in on his professional work. The carriage was propelled by mechanism operated by a man-servant by means of a treadle. The operator was placed on the rear of the carriage, and the occupant, seated in front, steered by a winch attached to a small wheel. This construction was frequently referred to by contemporaries of Richard, and even later on, and was copied by others during the following hundred years or so.

GOTTFRIED WILHELM VON LEIBNITZ

Born at Leipsic, Germany, July 6, 1646. Died at Hanover, November 14, 1716.

Leibnitz, in addition to his work as a philosopher and mathematician, was also interested in mechanics. He gave some attention to the study of the possibility of making improvements in common road vehicles, and he endeavored to encourage, though without results, his contemporary, Denis Papin.

HUMPHREY MACKWORTH

Born in 1647. Died in 1727.

A celebrated English politician and capitalist, Sir Humphrey Mackworth matriculated at Magdalene College, Oxford, December 11, 1674. He was entered at the Middle Temple, in June, 1675, and called to the bar in 1682. In 1695 he was engaged in developing collieries and copper and smelting works at Melencryddan, near Neath, Wales, and the improvements introduced by him there were of the greatest value. Among other improvements he constructed a wagon-way from the mines, and propelled his coal-carrying cars by sails.

Denis Papin

Born at Bloys, France, August 22, 1647. Died in England, 1712.

Papin was a son and nephew of a physician. He studied medicine in Paris and practiced for some time, attaining distinction in his profession. A passion for the sciences, mathematics and physics drew him away from medical practice and he became skillful in other lines. He followed assiduously the footsteps of Huygens and in some respects became a rival of his master in original thought and experimenting and in professional attainments.

Papin invented in 1698 a carriage that was fitted with a steam engine as such is now understood; that is, a cylinder and a piston. This was probably the first vehicle of its kind known in Europe. The construction was a model merely, a toy which ran around the room, but it is said to have worked well. Concerning this invention, Papin said: "I believe that one might use this invention for other things besides raising water. I have made a little model of a carriage that is propelled by this force. I have in mind what I can do, but I believe that the unevenness and turns of the highway will make this invention very difficult to perfect for carriages or road use." Although encouraged to prosecute his work by the Baron Gottfried Wilhelm von Leibnitz, his doubts could not be overcome in regard to the practicability of his proposed carriage. He still claimed, however, that by the aid of such vehicles, infantry could probably be moved as quickly as cavalry and without the necessity of heavy impedimenta of food and other supplies.

VAUCAUSON

A celebrated French mechanician, Vaucauson, in April, 1740, built a vehicle "to go without horses." He was visited at his palace in Rue Charonne, Paris, by King Louis Fifteenth, and the exhibition of this vehicle, which, according to reports, was propelled by a "simple watch spring," was reviewed in a journal of the time as follows:

"Yesterday, at 3 P. M. His Majesty, accompanied by several officers and high court functionaries, repaired to the palace of M. Vaucauson and took his seat on a species of throne specially prepared for his reception on a raised platform, whence he could clearly discern all the mechanism of the carriage in its gyrations through the avenues and alleys. The vehicle would seat two persons, and was painted scarlet, bordered in blue, ornamented with much gilding; the axle trees of the wheels were provided with brakes and set in motion by a fifth wheel, likewise well braked and bound with long ribbons of indented steel. Two chains communicated with a revolving lever in the hands of the conductor, who could at will start or stop the carriage without need of horses. His Majesty congratulated the skillful mechanician, ordering from him for his own use a similar vehicle to grace the royal stables. The Duke of Montemar, the Baron of Avenac and the Count of Bauzun, who had witnessed the trial, were unable to credit their own vision, so marvelous did the invention appear to them. Nevertheless, several members of the French Academy united in declaring that such a piece of mechanism could never circulate freely through the streets of any city."

Either from royal forgetfulness or thanks to the customary court intrigues to turn His Majesty from his purpose, or possibly because of the somewhat crude nature of the invention itself, the fact is that from that time forth not the slightest mention is to be found in history of the motor carriage of Vaucauson.

Robinson

It is on the authority of James Watt that Dr. Robinson is credited with having conceived the idea of driving carriages by steam power. Watt wrote as follows:

"My attention was first directed to the subject of steam engines by the late Dr. Robinson, then a student in the University of Glasgow, afterwards Professor of Natural Philosophy in the University of Edinburgh. He, in 1759, threw out the idea of applying the power of the steam engine to the moving of wheel carriages, and to other purposes, but the scheme was soon abandoned on his going abroad."

Erasmus Darwin

Born at Elton, Nottinghamshire, England, December 12, 1731. Died at Derby, April 18, 1802.

Having studied at St. John's College, Cambridge, and at Edinburgh, Darwin settled as a physician at Litchfield and gained a large practice. In 1781 he moved to Derby. He was a man of remarkable scientific attainments and a voluminous writer of poetry that was pervaded by enthusiasm and love of nature, but had little poetic quality.

Darwin wrote most of his poetry and evolved most of his ideas as he drove about the country in a doctor's covered sulky that was piled high with books and writing materials. He was in correspondence with Benjamin Franklin and Matthew Boulton about 1765 in regard to steam, and writing to Boulton, said: "As I was riding home yesterday I considered the scheme of the fiery chariot, and the longer I contemplated this favorite idea, the more practicable it appeared to me. I shall lay my thoughts before you, crude and undigested as they appeared to me, and by these hints you may be led into various trains of thinking upon this subject, and by that means (if any hints can assist your genius, which, without hints, is above all others I am acquainted with) be more likely to approve or disapprove. And as I am quite mad of the scheme, I hope you will not show this paper to anyone. These things are required: (1) a rotary motion; (2) easily altering its direction to any other direction; (3) to be accelerated, retarded, destroyed, revived, instantly and easily; (4) the bulk, the weight, the expense of the machine to be as small as possible in proportion to its weight." Darwin gave sketches and suggested that the steam carriage should have three or four wheels, and be driven by an engine having two cylinders open at the top, and the steam condensed in the bottom of the cylinder, on Newcomen's principle. The steam was to be admitted into the cylinders by cocks worked by the person in charge of the steering wheel, the injection cock being actuated by the engine. The "fiery chariot" never went beyond this suggestion, however.

Richard Lovell Edgeworth

An English gentleman of fortune, and much interested in mechanics, Richard Lovell Edgeworth was influenced by Dr. Erasmus Darwin to take up the subject of steam locomotion. In 1768, Dr. Small, in correspondence with James Watt, spoke of Edgeworth and his experiments in the problem of moving land and water carriages by steam. Two years later Edgeworth patented a portable railway system and then spent nearly forty years on that one idea.

When an old man of seventy, Edgeworth wrote to James Watt: "I have always thought that steam would become the universal lord, and that in time we should scorn the post horses." Dr. Smiles says: "Four years later he died, and left the problem which he had nearly all his life been trying ineffectually to solve, to be worked out by younger men."

Francis Moore

In 1769, Francis Moore, of London, a linen draper, invented a machine which he described as made of wood, iron, brass, copper, or other metals, and constructed upon peculiar principles, and capable of being wrought or put in motion by fire, water, or air, without being drawn by horses or any other beast or cattle; and which machines, or engines, upon repeated trials, he has discovered would be very useful in agriculture, carriage of persons and goods, either in coaches, chariots, chaises, carts, wagons, or other conveyances, and likewise in navigation, by causing ships, boats, barges, and other vessels to move, sail, or proceed, with more swiftness or despatch.

It was said that, so confident was the inventor of the success of his machine, he sold all his own horses, and by his advice many of his friends did the same, expecting that the price of that animal would be so affected by the invention, that it would not be again one-fourth of what it was then. Moore made several trials with his steam carriage, and took out three patents for it. Like many others of that time, however, Moore's carriages never got into use.

PLANTA

A Swiss army officer who was contemporary with Cugnot in the seventeenth century. He was engaged upon the problem of a steam road wagon at about the same time that Cugnot conceived and executed his vehicle in 1769. General Gribeauval, to whom Cugnot's plan had been referred, engaged Planta to pass upon it and to examine the new vehicle. The Swiss officer found it in all respects so much better than his own that he so reported to the French Ministry of War and abandoned further endeavors on that line.

J. S. KESTLER

In 1680 a description was published of a carriage designed by J. S. Kestler. This was merely a toy, set in motion by mercury in a tube heated by a candle.

BLANCHARD

In connection with his partner, Masurier, Blanchard brought out in Paris, in 1779, a vehicle that was somewhat patterned after the man-propelled carriage of Elié Richard. It was very successful and attracted a great deal of attention.

THOMAS CHARLES AUGUSTE DALLERY

Born at Amiens, France, September 4, 1754. Died at Jouy, near Versailles, in June, 1835.

About 1780, Dallery made a steam vehicle with a multi-tubular boiler which he claimed was an original invention of his own. This vehicle was run in Amiens and in 1790 was seen on the streets of Paris. In March, 1803, he secured a patent on the tubular boiler for use on his steamboat, or on his steam carriage. This vehicle was a boat-shaped wagon, driven by a steam engine.

JAMES WATT

Born at Greenock, Scotland, January 19, 1736. Died at Birmingham, Staffordshire, England, August 25, 1819.

Watt came of a respectable and industrious family. His grandfather was a professor of mathematics, while his father was an instrument maker, councillor and manufacturer. After a limited education young Watt went to London, in 1755, and became a mathematical and nautical instrument maker. In that capacity he became connected with Glasgow University, and there made his discoveries that resulted in the practical improvements in the steam engine which made him famous. He was associated with Matthew Boulton, under the firm name of Boulton & Watt, from 1774 to 1800, and the Watt engines that were built by that concern at Soho revolutionized England's mining industries. His steam engines represented a great step beyond the Newcomen engines, though still using low-pressure steam.

Watt's connection with steam carriages for use on the common roads, a subject that was of much moment in his day, was limited to a single patent and generally to discouraging the plans of others in that direction, owing to his fear that the introduction of high-pressure steam use would harm the engine business. In the patent granted to him in 1784 he proposed that the boiler of his carriage should be made of wooden staves, fastened with iron hoops, like a cask, and the furnace to be of iron, and placed in the inside of the boiler, surrounded with water.

Watt, however, never built the steam carriage. He retained the deepest prejudices against the use of high-pressure steam, saying: "I soon relinquished the idea of constructing an engine on this principle; from being sensible it would be liable to some of the objections against Savery's engine, viz., the danger of bursting the boiler, and also that a great part of the power of the steam would be lost, because no vacuum was formed to assist the descent of the piston."

Robert Fourness

Born in Otley, Yorkshire, England. Died at an early age.

Fourness became a practical engineer and invented several labor-saving machines. One of his first inventions was for a machine to split hides, that was set up and operated in the establishment of his father. Later in life he established works for himself in Sheffield, and afterwards in Gainsborough. In 1788, he was a resident of Elland, Halifax, and there made a steam carriage that was run by a three-cylinder inverted engine. Spur-gearing transmitted the driving power from the crank shaft to the axle. His patent was taken out in conjunction with James Ashworth. This vehicle was mounted on two driving wheels and had a smaller steering wheel in front.

GEORGE MEDHURST

Born at Shoreham, Kent, England, in February, 1759. Died in September, 1827.

Medhurst was educated as a clock maker, but in 1789 started as an engineer. In the same year he secured a patent for a windmill and pumps for compressing air to obtain motive power. One of the first investigators in this direction, the idea on which he worked and which continued to absorb his energy throughout life, was to make use of the wind when it served in order to compress large bodies of air for use when needed. In 1800, he took out a patent on an aeolian engine and demonstrated how carriages could be driven upon the common roads by compressed air stored in reservoirs underneath the body of the vehicle. He also contemplated applying this engine to other useful purposes and calculated that small carriages could be worked by a rotary engine and larger ones by reciprocating engines with special gear for varying power.

In describing his inventions and explaining his ideas regarding compressed air, Medhurst said: "The power applied to the machinery is compressed air, and the power to compress the air I obtain generally by wind, assisted and improved by machinery described in this specification, and in order to render my invention universally useful I propose to adapt my machinery and magazine so that it may be charged by hand, by a fall of water, by a vacuum obtained by wind and also by explosive and effervescent substances, for the rapid conveyance of passengers, mails, dispatches, artillery, military stores, etc., and to establish regular stage coaches and wagons throughout the kingdom, to convey goods and passengers, for public accommodation, by erecting windmills, water-mills, etc., at proper intervals upon the roads, to be employed in charging large magazines at these stations with compressed air, or in raising large magazines of water by wind, etc., by the power of which portable magazines may be charged when required by machinery for that purpose."

Medhurst contemplated establishing regular lines of coaches, with pumping stations at regular stopping places. He endeavored to form a company to work his inventions and develop his plans and published a pamphlet on the subject of compressed air. About 1800, he established himself as a machinist and ironmaster in Denmark street, Soho, and about ten years later was the first to suggest pneumatic tubes for the carriage of parcels or passengers. Some two years later he brought out the proposition for what has come to be known as the atmospheric railway, an appliance for conveying goods and passengers by the power of a piston in a continuous tube laid between the rails.

Andrew Vivian

A resident of Cornwall, England, Andrew Vivian, a cousin of Richard Trevithick, became much interested in the engineering experiments of his famous relative. He worked with his cousin and particularly assisted him in experiments on steam engines for propelling road carriages. In 1802, he was a joint patentee with Trevithick, in the early steam vehicle that was taken to London and was exhibited in that city, where for a short time it occasioned a great deal of public curiosity.

Du Quet

A Frenchman who, in 1714, designed a small windmill to give motion to the wheels of his carriages.

J. H. Genevois

A Swiss clergyman of the early part of the eighteenth century. He proposed to use windmills or sails on his wagon and by a system of springs to store the energy thus obtained until such time as it should be needed for driving purposes.

John Dumbell

In 1808, John Dumbell secured a patent for an engine that had many peculiar features. He planned to have the steam act on a series of vanes, or fliers, within a cylinder, "like the sails of a windmill," causing them to rotate together with the shaft to which they were fixed. Gearing transmitted the motion of this shaft to the driving wheels. The inventor proposed to raise steam by permitting water to drop upon a metal plate, kept at an intense heat by means of a strong fire, which was stimulated by a pair of bellows.

WILLIAM BRUNTON

Born at Dalkeith, Scotland, May 26, 1777. Died at Camborne, Cornwall, England, October 5, 1857.

The eldest son of Robert Brunton, a watch and clock maker, William Brunton studied mechanics first in his father's shop and then in England, under the guidance of his grandfather, who was a colliery viewer. When he was thirteen years of age, in 1790, he began work in the fitting shops of the New Lanark cotton mills of David Dale and Richard Arkwright. Remaining in that establishment for six years he then went to the Boulton & Watt shops, at Soho, where he was gradually promoted, until he finally became the foreman and superintendent of engine manufacturing.

In 1813, he went to the Jessop's Butterley Works, but remained there only three years, when he became a partner and mechanical manager of the Eagle Foundry, at Birmingham, a connection that he maintained for ten years. From 1825 to 1835, he was engaged in the practice of civil engineering in London. In the last-mentioned year, he became a share owner in the Cwm Avom tin works in Glamorganshire, Wales, where he superintended the erection of copper-smelting furnaces and rolling mills. He was also connected with the Maesteg Works in the same county and a brewery at Neath. Through the failure of these enterprises he lost the savings of his lifetime and was never again engaged actively in business. He invented many ingenious modes of reducing and manufacturing metals; made some of the original engines used on the Humber and the Trent and also some of the earliest that were seen on the Mersey, including those four vessels first operated on the Liverpool ferries in 1814. He also invented the calciner that was put in use in the tin mines at Cornwall and the silver ore works in Mexico.

Like nearly all the other engineers of his day, Brunton planned a steam carriage. This was built when he was at the Butterley Works, in 1813, and was called "the mechanical traveller." Although a peculiar machine it worked with some degree of success, at a gradient of one in thirty-six, all the winter of 1814, at the Newbottle Colliery. The machine was a steam horse rather than a steam carriage. It consisted of a curious combination of levers, the action of which nearly resembled that of the legs of a man in walking, with feet alternately made to press against the ground of the road or railway, and in such a manner as to adapt themselves to the various inclinations or inequalities of the surface. The feet were of various forms, the great object being to prevent them from injuring the road, and to obtain a firm footing, so that no jerks should take place at the return of the stroke, when the action of the engine came upon them; for this purpose they were made broad, with short spikes to lay hold of the ground. The boiler was a cylinder of wrought iron, five feet six inches long, three feet in diameter, and of such strength as to be capable of sustaining a pressure of upwards of four hundred pounds per square inch. The working cylinder was six inches in diameter, and the piston had a stroke of twenty-four inches; the step of the feet was twenty-six inches, and the whole machine, including water, weighed about forty-five hundredweight. In 1815, the engine of this carriage exploded and killed thirteen persons.

Thomas Tindall

A steam engine was patented, in 1814, by Thomas Tindall, of Scarborough. The inventor proposed to use this for an infinitude of purposes, such as driving carriages for the conveyance of passengers, ploughing land, mowing grass and corn, or working thrashing machines. The carriage had three wheels—one for steering. The steam engine drove, by spur gearing, four legs, which, pushing against the ground, moved the carriage. The engine could also be made to act upon the two hind wheels for ascending hills, or for drawing heavy loads. A windmill, driven partly by the action of the wind, and partly by the exhaust steam from the engine, was used as adjunct power.

John Baynes

A very ingenious modification of William Brunton's mechanical traveler, was the subject of a patent granted to John Baynes, a cutler, of Sheffield, England, in September, 1819. The mechanism was designed to be attached to carriages for the purpose of giving them motion by means of manual labor, or by other suitable power, and consisted of a peculiar combination of levers and rods. The patentee also stated that there might be several sets of the machinery above described for working each set with a treadle, or even only one set and treadle. Then he added: "I prefer two for ordinary purposes, particularly when only a single person is intended to be conveyed in the carriage, who may work the same by placing one foot on each treadle, in which the action will be alternate. The lower parts of the leg should be so formed or shod as not to slip upon the ground. This machinery may be variously applied to carriages, according to circumstances, so as that the treadles may be worked either behind or before the carriage, still producing a forward motion; in some cases it may be advantageous to joint the front end of the treadles to the carriage and press the feet on the hind ends."

JULIUS GRIFFITHS

Among those who came to the front with plans for steam carriages for the public highways, soon after the roads began to be improved, was Julius Griffiths, of Brompton Crescent. In 1821, he patented a steam carriage that was built by Joseph Bramhah, a celebrated engineer and manufacturer. It is said that part of the mechanism was designed by Arzberger, a foreigner.

The carriage has been termed by some English authorities "the first steam coach constructed in this country, expressly for the conveyance of passengers on common roads." It was repeatedly tested during a period of three or four years, but failed on account of boiler deficiencies. Alexander Gordon said of it: "The engines, pumps, and connections were all in the best style of mechanical execution, and had Mr. Griffiths' boiler been of such a kind as to generate regularly the required quantity of steam, a perfect steam carriage must have been the consequence." The carriage moved easily and answered very readily to guidance. The vehicle was a double coach and could carry eight passengers.

This locomotive had two vertical working steam cylinders, which with the boiler, condenser, and other details were suspended to a wood frame at the rear of the carriage. The engineer was seated behind and did his own firing. The boiler was a series of horizontal water tubes, one and one-half inches in diameter and two feet long; at each end the flanges were bolted to the vertical tubes forming the sides of the furnace. Attached to the wood frame in front of the driving wheels, was a small water tank, and a force pump supplied the boiler with water. The steam, passing through the cylinder, went into an air condenser. The power of the engines was communicated from the piston rods to the driving wheels of the carriage by sweep rods, the lower ends of which were provided with driving pinions and detents, which operated upon toothed gear fixed to the hind carriage axle. The object of this mechanism was to keep the driving pinions always in gear with the toothed wheels, however the engine and other machinery might vibrate or the wheels be jolted upon uneven ground. The boiler, engine, and other working parts were suspended to the wood frame by chain slings, having strong spiral springs so as to reduce the vibration from rough roads.

Edmund Cartwright

Born at Marnham, Nottinghamshire, England, April 24, 1743. Died at Hastings, October 30, 1823.

Cartwright was educated at Oxford and secured a living in the English church. He devoted himself to the ministry and to literature until 1784, when he became interested in machinery and in the following year invented the power loom. He took out other patents and also gave some attention to devising a mechanical carriage propelled by man power. In 1822, he made a vehicle that was moved by a pair of treadles and cranks worked by the driver.

Even the steam engine engaged his attention. Some improvements which he proposed in it are recorded in works on mechanics. While residing at Eltham, in Lincolnshire, he used frequently to tell his son that, if he lived to be a man, he would see both ships and land-carriages impelled by steam. At that early period he constructed a model of a steam engine attached to a barge, which he explained, about the year 1793, to Robert Fulton. It appears that even in his old age, only a year before his death, he was actively engaged in endeavoring to contrive a plan of propelling land-carriages by steam.

T. Burtsall

An engineer, of Edinburgh, Scotland, T. Burtsall, in conjunction with J. Hill, of London, got out, in 1824, a patent for flash or instantaneous generation boilers. His aim was to make the metal of the boiler store heat instead of a mass of water, and he accomplished this by heating the boiler to anywhere from two hundred and fifty degrees to six hundred degrees Fahrenheit, keeping the water in a separate vessel and pumping it into the boiler as steam was required. A coach that he built to run with this boiler weighed eight tons, and it was a failure, simply because the boiler could not make steam fast enough.

T. W. Parker

A working model of a light steam carriage was made by T. W. Parker, of Illinois, in 1825. Three wheels supported the carriage, the two hind wheels being eight feet in diameter. The double-cylinder engine was used.

George Pocock

One of the most curious of the wind vehicle productions that held the fancy of scientists to a slight extent in the early part of the nineteenth century was the charvolant or kite carriage that was devised by George Pocock in 1826, and built by Pocock and his partner, Colonel Viney. This was a very light one-seated carriage, drawn by a string of kites harnessed tandem. With a good wind these kites developed great power and it is said that the carriage whirled along, even on heavy roads, at the rate of a mile in three or even two and one-half minutes. Once Viney and Pocock made the trip from Bristol to London, and they often ran their carriage around Hyde Park and the suburbs of London. As the wind could not always be depended upon the charvolant was provided with a rear platform, upon which a pony was carried for emergencies.

Samuel Brown

In 1826, Samuel Brown applied his gas-vacuum engine to the propulsion of a carriage, which was effectively worked along the public roads in England. It even ascended the very steep acclivity of Shooter's Hill, in Kent, to the astonishment of numerous spectators. The expense of working this machine was, however, said far to exceed that of steam, and this formed a barrier to its introduction. Experiments with this engine for the propulsion of vessels on canals or rivers were also made by the Canal Gas Engine Company. Brown patented a locomotive for common roads in 1823.

JAMES NEVILLE

In January, 1827, James Neville, an engineer of London, took out a patent for a "new-invented improved carriage," to be worked by steam, the chief object of which appears to have been to provide wheels adapted to take a firm hold of the ground. He proposed to make each of the spokes of the wheels by means of two rods of iron, coming nearly together at the nave, but diverging considerably apart to their other ends, where they were fastened to an iron felly-ring of the breadth of the tire, and this tire was to be so provided with numerous pointed studs about half an inch long as to stick into the ground to prevent the wheel from slipping round. A second method of preventing this effect was to fasten upon the tire a series of flat springing plates, each of them forming a tangent to the circumference, so that as the wheels rolled forward each plate should be bent against the tire and recover its tangential position as it left the ground in its revolution. It was considered that the increased bearing surface of the plate, and the resistance of its farthest edge, would infallibly prevent slipping. For propelling the carriage Neville proposed to use a horizontal vibrating cylinder to give motion direct to the crank axis by means of the compound motion of the piston rod, as invented by Trevithick, the motion to the running wheels to be communicated through gear of different velocities.

T. S. Holland

Among the singular propositions for producing a locomotive action that were brought out early in the eighteenth century was that invented by T. S. Holland, of London, for which he took out a patent in December, 1827. The invention consisted in the application of an arrangement of levers, similar to that commonly known by the name of lazy-tongs, for the purpose of propelling carriages. The objects appeared to be to derive from the reciprocating motion of a short lever a considerable degree of speed, and to obtain an abutment against which the propellers should act horizontally, in the direction of the motion of the carriage, instead of obliquely to that motion, as is the case when carriages are impelled by levers striking the earth.

James Nasmyth

Born in Edinburgh, Scotland, August 19, 1808. Died in South Kensington, England, May 6, 1890.

While yet in his teens James Nasmyth showed great mechanical ability and constructed a small steam engine. In 1821, he became a student at the Edinburgh School of Arts. Six years later he had made a very substantial advance in his experiments. The story of what he endeavored to accomplish is best told by himself. In later life he wrote:

"About the year 1827, when I was nineteen years old, the subject of steam carriages to run upon common roads occupied considerable attention. Several engineers and mechanical schemers had tried their hands, but as yet no substantial results had come of their attempts to solve the problem. Like others, I tried my hand. Having made a small working model of a steam carriage, I exhibited it before the members of the Scottish Society of Arts. The performance of this active little machine was so gratifying to the Society, that they requested me to construct one of such power as to enable four or six persons to be conveyed along the ordinary roads. The members of the Society, in their individual capacity, subscribed three hundred dollars, which they placed in my hands as the means for carrying out their project. I accordingly set to work at once, and completed the carriage in about four months, when it was exhibited before the members of the Society of Arts. Many successful trials were made with it on the Queensferry Road, near Edinburgh. The runs were generally of four or five miles, with a load of eight passengers sitting on benches about three feet from the ground. The experiments were continued for nearly three months, to the great satisfaction of the members.

"I may mention that in my steam carriage I employed the waste steam to create a blast or draught, by discharging it into the short chimney of the boiler at its lowest part; and I found it most effective. I was not at that time aware that George Stephenson and others had adopted the same method; but it was afterwards gratifying to me to find that I had been correct as regards the important uses of the steam blast in the chimney. In fact, it is to this use of the waste steam that we owe the practical success of the locomotive engine as a tractive power on railways, especially at high speeds.

"The Society of Arts did not attach any commercial value to my road carriage. It was merely as a matter of experiment that they had invited me to construct it. When it proved successful they made me a present of the entire apparatus. As I was anxious to get on with my studies, and to prepare for the work of practical engineering, I proceeded no further. I broke up the steam carriage, and sold the two small high-pressure engines, provided with a strong boiler, for three hundred and thirty-five dollars, a sum which more than defrayed all the expenses of the construction and working of the machine."

F. Andrews

It is said that F. Andrews, of Stamford Rivers, Essex, England, was the inventor of the pilot steering wheel which was used by Gurney and has been often used since then. He also made other improvements in steam carriages in 1826. One of his patents was for the oscillating cylinders that were used by James Neville in his steam carriage. Andrews' steam carriage was a failure, like many others of that period, on account of imperfect working of the boiler.

Harland

Dr. Harland, of Scarborough, in 1827 invented and patented a steam carriage for running on common roads. A working model of the steam coach was perfected, embracing a multi-tubular boiler for quickly raising high-pressure steam, with a revolving surface condenser for reducing the steam to water again by means of its exposure to the cold draught of the atmosphere through the interstices of extremely thin laminations of copper plates. The entire machinery placed under the bottom of the carriage, was borne on springs; the whole being of an elegant form.

This model steam carriage ascended with ease the steepest roads. Its success was so complete that Harland designed a full-sized carriage; but the demands upon his professional skill were so great that he was prevented going further than constructing a pair of engines, the wheels, and a part of the boiler. Harland spent his leisure time in inventions and in that work was associated with Sir George Cayley. He was Mayor of Scarborough three times. He died in 1866.

PECQUEUR

Chief of shops at the Conservatoire des Arts et Metier, Paris, Pecqueur made a steam wagon in 1828. His vehicle had two drive wheels keyed to two pairs of axles. His planet gearing was the origin of the balance gear.

JAMES VINEY

Colonel James Viney, Royal Engineers, in 1829 patented a boiler intended for steam carriages. His plan was to have two, three, four, or six concentric hollow cylinders containing water, between which the fire from below passed up. An annular space for water, and an annular space or flue for the ascending fire, were placed alternately, the water being between two fires.

Chevalier Bordino

An Italian officer of engineers, Bordino devised and constructed a steam carriage for the diversion of his little daughter. It was a carriage à la Dumont, and for forty years was used regularly in the carnival festivities of Turin in the early part of the nineteenth century. It is still preserved as donated by the widow of Bordino to the Industrial Museum of Turin.

Clive

Best known as a writer of articles on the steam carriage, over the signature of Saxula, in the Mechanic's Magazine, Clive, of Cecil House, Staffordshire, England, also engaged in experimenting with steam. In 1830, he secured patents for two improvements in locomotives, one increasing the diameter of the wheels and the other increasing the throw of the cranks. After a time he seems to have lost faith in the steam carriage, for in 1843 he wrote: "I am an old common road steam carriage projector, but gave it up as impracticable ten years ago, and I am a warm admirer of Colonel Maceroni's inventions. My opinion for years has been, and often so expressed, that it is impossible to build an engine sufficiently strong to run even without a load on a common road, year by year, at the rate of fifteen to twenty miles an hour. It would break down. Cold iron at that speed cannot stand the shock of the momentum of a constant fall from stones and ruts of even an inch high."

Summers and Ogle

Two steam carriages built by Summers and Ogle, in 1831, were among the most successful vehicles of their kind in that day. One of these carriages had two steam cylinders, each seven and one-half inches in diameter and with eighteen-inch stroke. It was mounted on three wheels and its boiler would work at a pressure of two hundred and fifty pounds per square inch. Passengers were carried in the front and the middle of the coach, while the tank and the boiler were behind. The second carriage had three steam cylinders, each four inches in diameter, with a twelve-inch stroke. When the committee of the House of Commons was investigating the subject of steam locomotion on the common roads Summers and Ogle appeared and gave interesting particulars concerning their vehicles. The greatest velocity ever obtained was thirty-two miles an hour. They went from the turnpike gate at Southampton to the four-mile stone on the London road, a continued elevation, with one slight descent, at the rate of twenty-four and a half miles per hour, loaded with people; twenty passengers were often carried. Their first steam carriage ran from Cable Street, Wellclose Square, to within two miles and a half of Basingstoke, when the crank shaft broke, and they were obliged to put the whole machine into a barge on the canal and send it back to London. This same machine had previously run in various directions about the streets and outskirts of London. With their improved carriage they went from Southampton to Birmingham, Liverpool and London, with the greatest success.

The Saturday Magazine, of October 6, 1832, gave an account of one of their trials as follows: "I have just returned from witnessing the triumph of science in mechanics, by traveling along a hilly and crooked road from Oxford to Birmingham in a steam carriage. This truly wonderful machine is the invention of Captain Ogle, of the Royal Navy, and Mr. Summers, his partner, and is the first and only one that has accomplished so long a journey over chance roads, and without rails. Its rate of traveling may be called twelve miles an hour, but twenty or perhaps thirty down hill if not checked by the brake, a contrivance which places the whole of the machinery under complete control. Away went the splendid vehicle through that beauteous city (Oxford) at the rate of ten miles an hour, which, when clear of the houses, was accelerated to fourteen. Just as the steam carriage was entering the town of Birmingham, the supply of coke being exhausted, the steam dropped; and the good people, on learning the cause, flew to the frame, and dragged it into the inn yard."

GIBBS

An English engineer, Gibbs made a special study of the steam carriage of Sir Charles Dance in 1831. As a result of his investigations he built a steam drag in 1832. This was intended to draw passenger carriages and it had a boiler with spirally descending flue placed behind the driving wheels. In 1832, in conjunction with his partner, Applegate, he patented a steam carriage with a tubular boiler and oscillating engine cylinders. The power from the axle was transmitted to the driving wheels through friction bands, arranged in the bases of the wheels so that one or both wheels could be coupled to the axles.

CHARLES DANCE

An enthusiastic motorist, Sir Charles Dance, of London, in the first third of the ninteenth century did a great deal to encourage the engineers who were inventing steam road vehicles. He was financially interested in several of the companies that were organized to run steam coaches over the common roads. He was the backer of Goldsworthy Gurney, and was also engaged in building for himself. His most famous car was a coach that ran every day from the Strand, London, to Brighton. This was an engine mounted on four wheels with a tall rectangular funnel that narrowed toward the top. Above the engine were seats for six or seven persons besides the driver. Behind the engine was a vehicle like a boxcar, low hung on wheels. On the side of this box was emblazoned the coat of arms of its owner. On the roof seat in front were places for four passengers. On a big foot-board behind, stood the footman. This carriage was one of the spectacular sights of London at that time and great crowds gathered in the Strand every day to witness its departure.

Dance ran Gurney's coaches on the Cheltenham and Gloucester Road until public opposition compelled his withdrawal, but after that he was a joint patentee with Joshua Field, of an improved boiler. This was applied to the road carriage above mentioned and the first trips were made in September, 1833, with a drag and omnibus attached, a speed of sixteen miles an hour being attained. On the first trip from London to Brighton, fifteen passengers were carried and the distance of fifty-two miles was covered in five and a half hours, the return journey being performed in less than five hours. About the middle of October the steam drag and omnibus were put upon the road between Wellington Street, Waterloo Bridge, and Greenwich, where it continued to run for a fortnight, with a view of showing the public in London what could be done in this direction. The proprietor had no intention of making it a permanent mode of conveyance, and therefore kept the company as select as he could by charging half a crown for tickets each way.

JOSHUA FIELD

Born in 1786. Died in 1863.

A member of the well-known firm of Maudsley, Sons & Field, marine engineers, of London, England, Joshua Field took out a patent for an improved boiler, in conjunction with Sir Charles Dance. The firm made an improved vehicle for Dance, and in 1835 Field constructed for himself a steam carriage that made a trip in July with a party of guests. The carriage was driven up Denmark Hill, and did the distance, nine miles, in forty-four minutes. It also ran several times to Reading and back, at the rate of twelve miles an hour. One of the subscribers towards the building of this carriage, said that it was a success mechanically, but not economical. Field was one of the six founders of the Institution of Civil Engineers.

DIETZ

Previous to the time that the carriage of Francis Maceroni was taken to France, an engine designed by Dietz was run in the streets of Paris. In the reports of the Academy of Sciences and Academy of Industry in Paris, in 1840, this vehicle was described. The carriage had eight wheels, two of which were large and gave the impulsion. The six smaller wheels rose and fell according to the irregularity of the road, and at the same time assisted in bearing the weight of the carriages. The wheels were bound with wood tires, having cork underneath. The locomotive was a drag, drawing a carriage for passengers. The engine was of thirty horse-power, and a speed of ten miles an hour was made.

YATES

A steam carriage was built by Messrs. Yates & Smith, London, in 1834. It had a trial in July of that year, running from the factory in Whitechapel, along High and several other streets, at the rate of ten to twelve miles an hour. Vibrating engines, working on horizontal framing, were used. The coach resembled an ordinary stage-coach.

G. MILLICHAP

In a letter to an English engineering paper in 1837, G. Millichap, of Birmingham, claimed to have a locomotive carriage building. He wrote: "If your correspondent will take the trouble to call at my house I shall be happy to show him a locomotive carriage in a state of great forwardness, intended decidedly for common roads."

James Caleb Anderson

Born in Cork, Ireland, July 21, 1782. Died in London, April 4, 1861.

The father of Sir James Caleb Anderson, of Buttevant Castle, Ireland, was John Anderson, a celebrated merchant of Ireland, famous as the founder of the town of Fermoy. The son gave much attention to the subject of steam and steam propulsion, and made many experiments, taking out several patents. In 1831, he lodged a specification for improvements in machinery for propelling vessels on water; in 1837, for improvements in locomotive engines, and in 1846, for improvements in obtaining motive power and applying it to the propulsion of cars and vessels and the driving of machinery. His 1831 patent was for a manually-propelled vehicle, a carriage in which twenty-four men were arranged on seats, like rowers in a boat, but in two tiers, one above the other. The action was nearly the same as the pulling of oars, the only difference being that all the men sitting on one seat pulled at one horizontal cross-bar, each extremity of which was furnished with an anti-friction roller that ran between guide rails on the opposite sides of the carriage. The ends of each of these horizontal bars were connected to reciprocating rods that gave motion to a crank shaft, on which were mounted spur gear that actuated similar gear on the axis of the running wheels of the carriage; so that by sliding the gear on the axis of the latter any required velocity could be communicated to the carriage, or a sudden stop made. It was proposed to employ this as a drag, to draw one or more carriages containing passengers after it. The patentee had chiefly in view the movement of troops by this method.

Anderson gave financial support to W. H. James, in 1827, until he fell into pecuniary difficulties. Ten years later he re-engaged in steam carriage construction on his own account, and according to his own reports he expended over one hundred and fifty thousand dollars on experiments. It was said that he failed in twenty-nine carriages before he succeeded in the last. He patented a boiler that was said to be a poor copy of Walter Hancock's boiler. Then he organized a joint-stock company, the Steam Carriage and Wagon Company, which proposed to construct steam drags in Dublin and in Manchester, which, when completed, were to convey goods and passengers at double the speed and at half the cost of horse carriages.

Anderson said: "I produce and prove my steam drags before I am paid for them, and I keep them in repair; consequently, neither the public nor the company runs any risk. The first steam carriage built for the company is nearly completed. It will speak for itself." In the Mechanic's Magazine, June, 1839, a Dublin correspondent writes: "I was fortunate enough to get a sight of Sir James Anderson's steam carriage, with which I was much pleased. It had just arrived from the country, and was destined for London in about three weeks. The engine weighs ten tons, and will, I dare say, act very well. I shall have an opportunity of judging that, as the tender is at Cork. It has a sort of diligence, not joined, but to be attached to the tender, making in all three carriages. I talked a great deal about it to one of his principal men, who was most lavish in its praises, especially as regards the boiler." In August, 1839, the carriage arrived in London.

In 1840, a report said: "Several steam carriages are being built at Manchester and Dublin, under Sir James Anderson's patents, and one has been completed at each place. At Manchester the steam drag had been frequently running between Cross Street and Altrincham, and the last run was made at the rate of twenty miles an hour, with four tons on the tender, in the presence of Mr. Sharp, of the firm of Sharp, Roberts and Company, of Manchester, and others." A newspaper of the same year reported that an experimental trip of Anderson's steam drag for common roads took place on the Howth Road, Dublin. It ran about two hours, backing, and turning about in every direction—the object being chiefly to try the various parts in detail. It repeatedly turned the corners of the avenues at a speed of twelve miles an hour, the steam pressure required being only forty-six pounds per square inch. No smoke was seen, and little steam was observed. The whole machinery was ornamentally boxed in, so that none of the moving parts was exposed to view, and it was found that the horses did not shy at this carriage.

The company had great plans for travel communication by means of these drags between the chief towns in Ireland, as soon as a few of the steam carriages were finished. An even more pretentious scheme involved a service in conjunction with the railway trains from London, carriages to be run from Birmingham to Holyhead, whence passengers were to be conveyed to Dublin by steamer; from Dublin to

Galway the steam drags were to be employed; and thence to New York per vessel touching at Halifax; thus making Ireland the stepping-stone between England, Nova Scotia, and the United States of America. But all these plans came to naught.

Anderson continued to take out patents down to as late as 1858. He devoted more than thirty years of his life to the promotion of steam locomotion on common roads.

Robert Davidson

Robert Davidson, of Aberdeen, was probably the first to make an electrically propelled carriage large enough to carry passengers. This he did in 1839. His carriage could carry two persons when traveling over a fairly rough road, and though the prospects were enticing enough to cause investment in the enterprise, Davidson's subsequent work was on rail vehicles.

W. G. Heaton

W. G. and R. Heaton, of Birmingham, England, built several steam carriages which operated with various degrees of success in their neighborhood. Their patent was dated in October, 1830. The patent aimed particularly at the guidance of a locomotive carriage, and the management of the steam apparatus so that the power and speed might be accommodated to the nature of the road, the quantity of the load, and so on.

For the purpose of steering the carriage, a vertical spindle was placed at some distance before the axle of the front wheels and on its lower end a small drum was fixed. Around this drum was coiled a chain with its middle fixed upon the drum, and its ends made secure to the front axle formed a triangle with the drum, situated at the angle opposite the longest side. The other end of the vertical spindle was connected with a frame situated in front of the coachman's or rather the steersman's seat and here on the spindle was a horizontal beveled-toothed wheel. Over this wheel an axis extended, terminating in two crank handles proceeding from the axes in different directions, so that one was down when the other was up. Upon this axis was fixed another beveled-toothed wheel taking into the first. When these wheels were turned in one direction the right-hand fore wheel of the carriage advanced and the coach turned towards the left, while when they were turned in the other direction the left-hand wheel advanced and the carriage turned towards the right.

The driving wheels were connected with the axle by means of a pair of ratchets furnished with a double set of ratchet teeth and a reversing pall. By this one wheel could be advanced or backed while the other remained stationary, or moving in a contrary direction, an arrangement necessary for turning and backing. The steersman controlled the reversing pall by connecting rods and lever.

Motion was communicated to the driving wheels by a double set of spur wheel gear, arranged to give different powers or velocities, by having both a large and a small wheel fixed on the driving as well as the driven axis. By shifting the large wheel on the driving axis into gear with the small wheel on the driven axis speed was obtained, and by shifting their relative position till the small wheel on the driving axis came into gear with the large wheel on the driven axis, power was obtained at the expense of speed. These two axes were kept at the same distance from each other by means of connecting rods, although the relative positions might be changed by the motion of the carriage on rough roads.

In August, 1833, the Heatons placed a steam drag on the road between Worcester and Birmingham. A slight accident occurred at the start, but after repairs were made the trial was a success. Attached to the engine was a stage-coach, carrying twenty passengers, the load weighing nearly two tons. Lickey Hill was ascended, a rise of one in nine, and even one in eight in some places. Many parts of the hill were very soft, but by putting both wheels in gear they ascended to the summit, seven hundred yards in nine minutes. A company was formed in Birmingham to construct and run these carriages, subject to the condition of keeping up an average speed of ten miles an hour. A new carriage was built and tried in 1834, but after trials, the Messrs. Heaton dissolved their contract, as they were unable to do more than seven or eight miles an hour. After spending upwards of ten thousand dollars in endeavors to effect steam traveling, they retired from the field, stating that the wear and tear were excessive at ten miles an hour, and that the carriage was heavy, and wasteful in steam.

F. Hill

An English engineer, connected with the Deptford Chemical Works, Hill was among the first to be interested in steam-road locomotion. He was familiar with Hancock's experiments and made a carriage of his own that was tried in 1840. He journeyed to Sevenoaks and elsewhere and ran up steep hills with the carriage, fully loaded, at twelve miles an hour, and on the level at sixteen miles an hour. He adopted the compensating gear that was invented by Richard Roberts and that by some writers has been credited to him.

To put Hill's patents to practical use The General Steam Carriage Company was formed in 1843. The probable success of the company was based upon the belief that there was a demand for additional road accommodations in order that road locomotion should counteract the exorbitant charges made by the gigantic railway monopoly for conveying goods short distances. The company stated in its prospectus "that while they confidently believe the improved steam coach which they have engaged and propose to employ in the first instance to be the most perfect now known in England, they do not bind themselves to adhere to any particular invention, but will avail themselves of every discovery to promote steam coach conveyance."

Trial trips were made on the Windsor, Brighton, Hastings, and similar roads, and with success. Once the carriage made a trip to Hastings and back, a distance of one hundred and twenty-eight miles, in one day, half the time occupied by the stage coaches. The Mechanic's Magazine said: "We accompanied Hill, about a year ago, in a short run up and down the hills about Blackheath, Bromley, and neighborhood; and we had again the pleasure of accompanying him in a delightful trip, on the Hastings Road, as far as Tunbridge and back. The manner in which his carriage took all the hills, both in the ascent and the descent, proved how completely every difficulty on this head had been surmounted."

In the Hill carriage, both the coach and the machinery were erected upon a strong frame mounted upon substantial springs. In the rear were the boiler, furnace, and water tanks, with a place for the engineer and fireman. In front was a coach body with seats for six inside, three on the box, and the conductor in front. The front part of the carriage was also suspended upon springs. The carriage was propelled by a pair of ten-inch cylinders and pistons, horizontally placed beneath the carriage. These acted upon two nine-inch cranks, coupled to the main axle through compensating gear; the two six-foot six-inch diameter driving wheels had the full power of the engines passed through them. The weight of the boiler when empty was two thousand three hundred pounds, and it had a capacity of about sixty gallons of water, while one hundred gallons more were contained in the tanks. The total weight of the carriage, including water, coke, and twelve passengers, was less than four tons. On heavy and rough roads the steam pressure was seventy pounds per square inch, but on good roads only sixty pounds. The average speed was sixteen miles an hour, but on a level twenty miles an hour was reached. As late as 1843, Hill's carriages were running from London to Birmingham, having been in operation four or five years. Smooth in motion, they carried their passengers comfortably, but soon went out of use.

GOODMAN

Early in the forties a small road locomotive was made by Goodman, of Southwark, London. It was worked by a pair of direct-acting engines, coupled to the crank shaft. A chain pinion on the crank shaft transmitted motion to the main axle through an endless pitch chain working over a chain wheel of larger diameter on the driving shaft. The smoke from the boiler was conducted by a flue placed beneath the carriage. The vehicle had a speed of from ten to twelve miles an hour.

NORRGBER

A correspondent of The Mechanic's Magazine, of London, wrote in 1843: "Norrgber, of Sweden, a locksmith and an ingenious mechanic, made a steam carriage which ran between Copenhagen and Corsoer, carrying thirty passengers, the engine being of eight horse-power."

J. K. FISHER

A small steam carriage, that in general character was like a railroad locomotive, was designed by J. K. Fisher, of New York, in 1840. It was not until 1853, however, that he went beyond this. Then he built another carriage, with driving wheels five feet in diameter, and two steam cylinders four inches in diameter, with ten-inch stroke. This carriage attained a speed of fifteen miles an hour on good pavements. During the next two years, Fisher made many trips, sometimes running twelve miles an hour without excessive wear. In his later engines he introduced several novelties, among them being parallel connections between the crank shaft and the driving axle. In the steering gear a screw was placed across the front part of the carriage carrying a nut, to which the end of an elongated reverted pole was jointed. The screw was turned by bevel gearing, one wheel being keyed to the end of the screw, and the other to the steerage rod, the opposite end of this rod having a lever placed within easy access of the footplate. Fisher's carriages were driven by direct-acting engines, one cylinder on each side of the smoke-box.

R. W. Thompson

Born in Stonehaven, England, in 1822. Died, March 8, 1873.

R. W. Thompson came to the United States in early life, but returned to England and engaged in scientific experimenting and studying, and in engineering at Aberdeen and Dundee. He invented a rotary engine during this period of his life. In 1846, being then in business for himself, he conceived the idea of india-rubber tires and perfected this in 1876. In December of that year he made a small road locomotive to draw an omnibus and this was sent to the Island of Ceylon. Other road steamers of Thompson's design were manufactured and sent to India and elsewhere.

Anthony Bernhard

In 1848, a compressed-air carriage invented by Anthony Bernhard, Baron von Rathen, was built in England. It weighed three tons, and on its first trip was driven at a speed of eight miles an hour. Upon one occasion it made twelve miles an hour on a trip from Putney to Wandsworth, carrying twenty passengers. Until near 1870, Baron von Rathen was engaged in inventing compressed-air engines.

BATTIN

In 1856, Joseph Battin, of Newark, N. J., constructed a steam carriage with a vertical boiler and oscillating engines.

RICHARD DUDGEON

A small locomotive for the common roads was built in 1857, by Richard Dudgeon, an engineer, of New York. It had two steam cylinders, each three inches in diameter and with sixteen-inch stroke, and drew a light carriage at ten miles an hour on gravel roads. The carriage was destroyed by fire at the New York Crystal Palace in 1858. Dudgeon is said to have afterward built another carriage, which was larger and more clumsy than the other. A few years ago this was discovered in an old barn in Locust Valley, L. I. It was fixed up and started out and demonstrated that, old as it was, it could go at a speed of more than ten miles an hour.

LOUGH AND MESSENGER

In 1858, Messrs. Lough and Messenger, of Swindon, England, designed and erected a steam-road locomotive which for two years ran at fifteen miles an hour on level roads, and six miles an hour up grades of one in twenty. The engine had two cylinders, each three and one-half inches in diameter and with five-inch stroke, working direct on to the crank axle. The driving wheels were three and one-half feet in diameter, and the leading wheels two feet in diameter. The vertical boiler fixed on the frame was worked at one-hundred-and-twenty-pound pressure. The tanks held forty gallons of feed water. The total weight of the locomotive was eight hundred pounds.

Thomas Rickett

When the revival of interest in the common-road steam locomotive began in England, about 1857, Thomas Rickett, of Castle Foundry, Buckingham, was one of the first to give attention to the subject. He built a road locomotive in 1858 for the Marquis of Stafford. This engine had two driving wheels and a steering wheel. The boiler was at the back with the steam cylinders horizontally on each side of it. Three passengers were carried.

The carriage was steered by means of a lever connected with the fork of the front wheel. The cylinders were three inches in diameter, with nine-inch stroke; the working steam pressure was one hundred pounds per square inch. The driving wheels were three feet in diameter. The weight of the carriage when fully loaded was only three thousand pounds. On level roads the speed was about twelve miles an hour.

An account of one of the trips in 1859 was as follows in the columns of The Engineer: "Lord Stafford and party made another trip with the steam carriage from Buckingham to Wolverton. His lordship drove and steered, and although the roads were very heavy, they were not more than an hour in running the nine miles to Old Wolverton. His lordship has repeatedly said that it is guided with the greatest ease and precision. It was designed by Mr. Rickett to run ten miles an hour. One mile in five minutes has been attained, at which it was perfectly steady, the centre of gravity being not more than two feet from the ground. A few days afterwards this little engine started from Messrs. Hayes' Works, Stoney Stratford, with a party consisting of the Marquis of Stafford, Lord Alfred Paget, and two Hungarian noblemen. They proceeded through the town of Stoney Stratford at a rapid pace, and after a short trip returned to the Wolverton railway station. The trip was in all respects successful, and shows beyond a doubt that steam locomotion for common roads is practicable."

Two other engines were built by Rickett, one of them for the Earl of Caithness. Some improvements were installed in this carriage, which was intended to carry three passengers. The weight of the carriage, fully loaded, was five thousand pounds.

In this carriage, the Earl of Caithness traveled from Inverness to his seat, Borrogill Castle, within a few miles of John o' Groat's House. He describes his trip as follows: "I may state that such a feat as going over the Ord of Caithness has never before been accomplished by steam, as I believe we rose one thousand feet in about five miles. The Ord is one of the largest and steepest hills in Scotland. The turns in the road are very sharp. All this I got over without trouble. There is, I am confident, no difficulty in driving a steam carriage on a common road. It is cheap, and on a level I got as much as nineteen miles an hour." The Earl of Caithness brought the trial to a successful result, and some expert authorities jumped to the conclusion that at once steam traveling upon the high roads of England would be availed of to a large extent; but that did not happen.

In 1864, Mr. Rickett furnished an engine for working a passenger and light goods service in Spain, intended to carry thirty passengers up an incline of one in twelve, at ten miles an hour. The steam cylinders were eight inches in diameter, and the driving wheels four feet in diameter. The boiler would sustain a pressure of two hundred pounds. Rickett's later engines had spur wheels; but his last engines were direct-acting. In November, 1864, he says: "The direct-acting engines mount inclines of one in ten easily; whether at eight, four, two, or one mile an hour, on inclines with five tons behind them, they stick to their work better than geared engines."

DANIEL ADAMSON

In 1858 the firm of Daniel Adamson & Co., of Dukinfield, near Manchester, England, built a common-road locomotive for a Mr. Schmidt. A multitubular boiler was used, two and one-half feet in diameter and five and one-half feet long, with a working pressure of one hundred and fifty pounds per square inch. The engine, which weighed five thousand six hundred pounds and was borne on three wheels, was calculated to run at eight miles an hour. A steam cylinder of six-inch diameter was attached to each side of the locomotive, and these cylinders actuated a pair of driving wheels three feet six inches in diameter.

Mr. Schmidt gave this vehicle a thorough trying out and especially raced it with several competitors.

On one of these races, in 1867, with a Boulton steam carriage, the start was made from Ashton-under-Lyne, for the show ground at Old Trafford, a distance of over eight miles. Although the Adamson engine was the larger, the smaller one easily passed it during the first mile, and kept a good lead all the way, arriving at Old Trafford under the hour.

Mr. Schmidt sent his road locomotive to the Havre Exhibition, in 1868, and a trial of its powers was made by French engineers, and M. Nicole, director of the exhibition. Mr. Schmidt conducted the engine himself, and to it was attached an omnibus containing the commissioners. The engine and carriage traversed several streets of Havre and mounted a sharp incline. Other trips were made to several villages in the neighborhood of the exhibition, and the engine behaved very satisfactorily.

STIRLING

In a road steamer designed by Stirling, of Kilmarnock, in 1859, the five traveling wheels were mounted upon springs. A single wheel was used as a driver, and more or less weight was thrown upon this wheel. The leading and trailing wheels swiveled in concert, in opposite directions, by means of right and left hand worms and worm wheels. The carriage was thus made to move in a curve of comparatively short radius.

W. O. CARRETT

In 1860, George Salt, of Saltshire, England, employed W. O. Carrett, of the firm of Carrett, Marshall & Co., proprietors of the Gun Foundry at Leeds, to design and build a steam pleasure carriage for him. The carriage was first shown and exhibited at the Royal Show held in Leeds, 1861, and likewise at the London Exhibition, 1862. It had two steam cylinders, six inches in diameter and with eight-inch stroke. The boiler was of the locomotive multitubular type, two feet six inches in diameter, and five feet three inches long. It had a working pressure of one hundred and fifty pounds per square inch, the test pressure being three hundred pounds. The locomotive was mounted upon two driving wheels, each four feet in diameter, made of steel, and a leading wheel was three feet in diameter. Seats were provided for nine persons, including the steerer and the fireman. The traveling speed was fifteen miles an hour; and the weight of the carriage, fully loaded, was five tons. Motion was communicated from the crank shaft to the driving axle through spur gearing.

The English magazine, Engineering, in an article in June, 1866, said: "This steam carriage, made by Carrett, Marshall & Co., was probably the most remarkable locomotive ever made. True, it did little good for itself as a steam carriage, and its owner at last made a present of it—much as an Eastern prince might send a friend a white elephant—to that enthusiastic amateur, Mr. Frederick Hodges, who christened it the Fly-by-Night, and who did fly, and no mistake, through the Kentish villages when most honest people were in their beds. Its enterprising owner was repeatedly pulled up and fined, and to this day his exploits are remembered against him." Hodges ran the engine eight hundred miles; he had six summonses in six weeks, and one was for running the engine thirty miles an hour. It was afterwards altered to resemble a fire engine and the passengers were equipped like firemen, wearing brass helmets. The device did not deceive the police, and finally the carriage was made over into a real self-moving fire engine.

RICHARD TANGYE

The steam carriage built by the Tangye Brothers, of England, about 1852, was a simple affair. It had seating capacity in the body for six or eight persons, while three or four more could be accommodated in front. The driver who sat in front had full control of the stop valve and reversing lever, so that the engine could be stopped or reversed by him as occasion required. The speed of twenty miles an hour could be attained, and the engine with its load easily ascended the steepest gradients.

Richard Tangye, in his autobiography, speaks of his experience with this carriage in the following terms: "Great interest was manifested in our experiment, and it soon became evident that there was an opening for a considerable business in these engines, and we made our preparations accordingly, but the 'wisdom' of Parliament made it impossible. The squires became alarmed lest their horses should take fright; and although a judge ruled that a horse that would not stand the sight or sound of a locomotive, in these days of steam, constituted a public danger, and that its owner should be punished and not the owner of the locomotive, an act was passed providing that no engine should travel more than four miles an hour on the public roads. Thus was the trade in quick-speed locomotives strangled in its cradle; and the inhabitants of country districts left unprovided with improved facilities for traveling." The Tangye carriage thus driven out of England was sent to India, where it continued to give good service.

T. W. COWAN

At the London Exhibition of 1862, the Messrs. Yarrow and Hilditch, of Barnsbury, near London, exhibited a steam carriage, designed and made by T. W. Cowan, of Greenwich. Eleven passengers, besides the driver and the fireman, were carried and the vehicle with full load weighed two tons and a half. The boiler, of steel, was a vertical multitubular two feet in diameter and three feet nine inches high. The frame of the carriage was of ash, lined with wrought-iron plates, and to the outside of the bottom sill were two iron foundation plates, to which the cylinders and other parts were attached. The cylinders were five inches in diameter and had nine-inch stroke.

CHARLES T. HAYBALL

A quick-speed road locomotive was made by Charles T. Hayball, of Lymington, Hants, England, in 1864. The machinery was mounted upon a wrought-iron frame, that was carried upon three wheels. The two driving wheels had an inner and an outer tire, and the space between was filled with wood to reduce noise and lessen the concussion. The two steam cylinders were each four and one-half inches in diameter and with six-inch stroke. Hayball used a vertical boiler, two feet two inches in diameter, and four feet high, working at a pressure of one hundred and fifty pounds. The carriage ran up an incline of one in twelve at sixteen miles an hour, and traveled four miles an hour in fourteen minutes, up hill and down, with ten passengers on board.

Isaac W. Boulton

In August, 1867, Thomas Boulton says: "I ran a small road locomotive constructed by Isaac W. Boulton, of Ashton-under-Lyne, from here through Manchester, Eccles, Warrington, Preston Brook, to Chester, paraded the principal streets of Chester, and returned home, the distance being over ninety miles in one day without a stoppage except for water." Boulton's engine had one cylinder four and one-half inches in diameter, and with nine-inch stroke. The boiler worked at one hundred and thirty pounds pressure per square inch. The driving wheels were five feet in diameter. Two speeds were obtained by means of spur gearing between the crank shaft and the counter shaft. On the Chester trip six persons, and sometimes eight and ten passengers, were carried.

Armstrong

The virtues of the horseless vehicle early penetrated to India. Many English manufacturers sent carriages there. Some time in 1868, a steam carriage, with two steam cylinders, each three inches in diameter, and with six-inch stroke, was made by Armstrong, of Rawilpindee, Punjab. A separate stop valve was fitted to each cylinder. The boiler was fifteen inches in diameter and three feet high, and worked steam pressure of one hundred pounds per square inch. Twelve miles an hour on the level, and six miles an hour up grade of one in twenty, were made. The driving wheels were three feet in diameter.

PIERRE RAVEL

Ravel, of France, planned in 1868 a steam vehicle, and about 1870 completed the construction of one at the barracks at Saint-Owen. Then came the declaration of war with Prussia, and the barracks, being within the zone of fortification, the vehicle was lost or destroyed. There is no certainty that it was ever unearthed after peace was declared.

L. T. PYOTT

Before 1876, a motor vehicle was invented by L. T. Pyott, who was then a foreman with the Baldwin Locomotive Works in Philadelphia. The carriage, which could carry seven persons at the rate of twenty miles an hour, cost about two thousand two hundred dollars, and weighed nearly two tons. It was shown at the Centennial Exposition in Philadelphia in 1876, but was not allowed to run on the streets.

A. RICHTER

An engineer and mechanician of Neider-Bielan, Oberlaneitz, Germany, Richter secured in 1877 a patent for a vehicle that was propelled by a motor consisting of a stack or battery of elliptic springs horizontally disposed, which were compressed by a charge of powerful powder exploded in what was practically a cannon. The subsequent expansion transmitted the driving effort to the wheels by a rack of gears. The success of this vehicle is not generally known.

RAFFARD

In 1881, Raffard, a French engineer, made a tricycle and a tram-car that is said to have been the first electric automobile which ran satisfactorily.

CHARLES JEANTEAUD

It is claimed for Jeanteaud that he built a four-wheeled electric vehicle about 1881, which was changed in 1887 by the addition of an Immisch motor. In 1890 he constructed a three-wheeled steam vehicle for five persons, having the advice and interest of Archdeacon. In June, 1895, at the Paris-Bordeaux race, he entered an electric automobile and established battery relays every twenty-five kilometers, but without success so far as speed was involved in comparison with the gasoline cars. In 1897 he constructed a gasoline phaeton, but his subsequent work has been primarily confined to the electric.

SYLVESTER HAYWOOD ROPER

As early as 1850, Sylvester Haywood Roper, of Roxbury, Mass., began experimenting with steam for street-vehicle propulsion. In 1882, when he was seventy-three years of age, he fitted a Columbia bicycle with a miniature engine, and with this he could run seventy miles on one charge of fuel. His bicycle weighed one hundred and sixty-five pounds. He engaged in many track events and his record for three runs of one-third of a mile each, was forty-two, thirty-nine and thirty-seven seconds.

COPELAND

A tandem tricycle with a vertical boiler and a two-cylinder vertical engine was built by Copeland, of Philadelphia, in 1882. Kerosene was used to fire the boiler. It is said that over two hundred of these machines were built.

G. BOUTON

An ingenious and practical engineer, Bouton made various mechanical devices, but it is claimed that from a clever toy came the associations which have resulted in the now famous firm, DeDion-Bouton, with which he is connected. It is said Compte DeDion saw this toy and on asking for the maker, met Bouton. Thus came the partnership, in 1882, with Bouton and Trepardoux. Bouton made a steam tricycle in 1884, containing the remarkable light and efficient boiler of his invention, which for years remained the most important contribution of the firm to this art. In 1885 a quadricycle was made, and the success attending the runs made with this, in which Merrelle co-operated, was such as to bring forth the personal ideas of DeDion in so strong a manner that Trepardoux and Merrelle severed their connections with the firm.

The real beginning of the work of this firm was in 1884, and the several years following saw the production of numerous steam machines, including phaetons, dog carts, and a variety of other types.

Even as late as 1897 heavy steam chars-bancs were made by them, and that year also saw their well-known thirty-five-passenger, six-wheeled coach, Pauline, on the streets of Paris—a vehicle which cost over twenty-six thousand francs, and had a thirty-five horse-power steam tractor. This vehicle had been preceded by a somewhat similar one constructed in 1893 on the old idea of a mechanical horse attached to an ordinary 'bus body from which the front wheels had been removed.

In 1895, DeDion-Bouton produced their first liquid hydro-carbon engine vehicle—a tricycle with air-cooled motor and dry-battery ignition, which is so well known to everyone in the industry to-day. These were manufactured in large numbers, and were followed by larger gasoline vehicles into which they introduced their engine, namely, a vertical position. In 1899, their three-passenger, four-wheeled vehicle, and in 1900 a six-passenger vehicle, made good reputations. Since then their large factory at Putaux, France, well known under the name of DeDion-Bouton et Cie, has been continually crowded with work on vehicles, and with the manufacture of their motors which are still sold independently to other makers in France, as well as in other countries. In fact the manufacture of engines and parts might be said to be now their main work.

Count A. DeDion

Count DeDion's interest in an ingenious mechanical device constructed by Bouton, led to his backing the enterprise now so well known under his name. His activity in the Automobile Club of France, and in all the sporting events in the past ten years, has in fact brought him into far more prominence than his associate, Bouton. His interest and energy in connection with his company are well known, and though the credit for the mechanical work must undoubtedly be given to Bouton, DeDion is largely responsible for the great success and general prominence of the company.

Armand Peugeot

In 1885, and again in 1889, Armand Peugeot, a French inventor and manufacturer, brought up the subject of automobiles, and in 1889 he began to manufacture, using the Daimler motor. His first attention having been given to the motor, he brought out very soon his famous two-parallel cylinder mounted horizontally on the body frame. Originally of the firm of Fils de Peugeot, he severed his connection with that firm, and in 1876 formed the Society of Artisans. In 1898, additional factories were erected at Fives-Lille, and now the concern has works also at Audincourt. The latter works is claimed to be the most extensive automobile manufacturing establishment in the world. Peugeot is a member of many learned societies, was elected an officer of the Academie in 1881, and a Chevalier of the Legion of Honor in 1889.

Radcliffe Ward

Ward commenced his experiments in England about 1886, and built a cab in 1887, which he ran in Brighton with more or less success. A second vehicle, an omnibus, was built by him and run on the streets in London in 1888, and actually covered, all told, five thousand miles.

MORS

A manufacturer of electrical apparatus, the Mors establishment made a steam vehicle in 1886, and some ten years later began to manufacture gasoline vehicles.

MAGNUS VOLK

In 1887, Volk built an electrical dog cart which, like that of Ward, was seen on the streets of Brighton. The next year he associated himself with Immisch & Co., and built for the Sultan of Turkey an electrical dog cart. This was claimed to have a radius of fifty miles at ten miles an hour, with seven hundred pounds of battery in twenty-four cells, driving the vehicle by means of a one horse-power motor.

BUTLER

About the same time that Daimler and Benz were at work, Butler, an Englishman, was studying to make a hydro-carbon engine. He had drawings in 1884 and got out a patent in 1887. He built a tricycle soon after that date. This had two front wheels as steering wheels and a rear wheel driven by a two-cylinder engine. But Butler did not carry his plans further, for, as he wrote in 1890, "the authorities do not countenance its use on roads, and I have abandoned in consequence any further development of it."

LE BLANT

The steam carriage that Le Blant, of France, built carried nine passengers, and its weight, fuel and water included, was three and one-half tons. The engine was three-cylinder horizontal, and the boiler, a Serpollet instantaneous generator, was placed behind the carriage, the fireman beside it and the driver in front.

EMILE DELAHAYE

Delahaye, of Tours, associated himself with the firm of Cail in 1870, spending some years in Belgium, but in 1890 the automobile so attracted him as to lead him to the construction of his first vehicle. For ten years he practically adhered to the horizontal engine under the seat, which construction we find him using in 1900. It is worthy of note that to Delahaye is given credit for the practical adaptation of the radiator in the arrangement now generally used in the cooling system.

ROGER

Roger, of Paris, was the French licensee for Benz, taking up that motor much in the same manner as Panhard & Levassor took up the Daimler. In fact he had such close relations with Benz as to guide the further development of both. To this extent he was doubtless largely responsible for converting Benz to the four-cycle instead of the two-cycle construction, and he is also credited with having brought about the change from the vertical crank shaft to the horizontal in the Benz cars. Making good headway in 1894, he had produced fifty or more machines by 1895, and ran one in the Paris-Bordeaux race of that year. He brought a car to New York in 1896, and took part in the Cosmopolitan race, from New York to Ardsley and return.

GEORGES RICHARD

In 1893, Georges Richard began cycle manufacturing in a small shop and two years later turned his business into a limited corporation. In 1897, he began the manufacture of automobiles. His motor is a development of the Benz, with ignition improvement.

POCHAIN

Pochain, in France, built in 1893 a six-seated phaeton with fifty-four cells of battery, which would seem to have been practically the first satisfactory vehicle of its kind.

LOUIS KRIEGER

Early in the nineties of the last century Krieger made an electric vehicle. About 1894, he introduced his four-passenger hack, converted by substituting an electric fore carriage for the front axle of an ordinary vehicle. He has since developed his electric vehicles in the class of city carriages. A touring car, built for England, called the Powerful, made in 1901 notable records in that country in a long tour through the Isles. The principal work of Krieger, however, has been in the development of front drive and steer construction.

DEDETRICH

Baron DeDetrich is of the well-known house that claims to have been founded more than one hundred years ago in Luneville, Alsace, and has grown to be one of the greatest works for the manufacture of locomotives and other machinery. In 1880 the concern is said to have employed four thousand men. Its connection with the automobile industry began practically in 1895, when the construction of automobiles on the system of Amédèe Bollèe & Sons was undertaken. With large resources and ability development was naturally rapid, resulting in the production to-day of one of the first-class French makes.

DAVID SALOMONS

Sir David Salomons, Bart., was born in England, in 1851. He was educated for a short period at University College, London, and afterwards at Caius College, Cambridge, where he was graduated with natural science honors. He is a member of the Institution of Electrical Engineers, where he took leading part for many years on the Council, and served in the positions of honorary treasurer and vice-president. He is a fellow of the Royal Astronomical Society, of the Physical Society of London, and of the Royal Microscopical Society, and an associate of the Institution of Civil Engineers.

Sir David was one of the first in England to adopt the electric light. This was about the year 1874, when he found it necessary to make the lamps, switches and other apparatus himself, as those were unobtainable at the time; much of the apparatus in general use to-day has been copied from his models. About 1874-5, he constructed a small electrical road carriage, which was in use a short time only, owing to the trouble of re-charging batteries, as no accumulators existed at that period. Devoting himself largely to scientific investigation he is the author of various works on scientific subjects, such as photographic optical formulæ, photography and electrical subjects, his chief work being his three-volume Electric Light Installations, now entering its ninth edition. Of this work, the first volume on Accumulators was for a great many years the only practical work on the subject. He is also the author of many papers read before scientific societies, including the Royal Society and Royal Institution. He is an original member of the Automobile Club of France and of the Automobile Club of Great Britain, being a member of the committee of the former and member of committee and a vice-president of the latter, and is also an ordinary or honorary member of most of the Continental automobile clubs. He was Mayor of Tunbridge Wells, 1894-5, and High Sheriff of Kent in 1881, and is a Magistrate for Kent, Sussex, Middlesex, Westminster and London.

The connection of Sir David Salomons with the encouragement and development of self-propelled traffic in the United Kingdom, constitutes one of the most important chapters in the contemporaneous history of the automobile. His first step to secure a favorable public opinion for the legislative measures that he proposed was to have an exhibition of vehicles, which took place at Tunbridge Wells, in October, 1895. As a result of this exhibition and a voluminous correspondence thereafter, the newspapers of Great Britain and many of the members of the Houses of Lords and Commons were brought to see the justice of the measures asked for. Next, the Self-Propelled Traffic Association was organized. Sir David Salomons was elected president and the campaign for Parliamentary action was inaugurated and brilliantly and energetically prosecuted. When the bill came before the Commons and the Lords it was substantially supported, but its provisions received a great deal of discussion. Some amendments, particularly relating to the questions of smoke and petroleum use, were attached to it. In the end, however, the act that was passed was generally satisfactory to all interested in the promotion and protection of self-propelled traffic. It has been said that "there has hardly been an act passed containing more liberal clauses and with more unity of action." Its provisions allow of reasonable travel of all kinds of self-propelled vehicles throughout the Kingdom and the act as a whole is regarded as one of the most notable advances made in this matter during the present generation.

Leon Bollèe

A brother of Amédèe Bollèe, Leon Bollèe has been long interested in the business that bears the family name. In 1896, he brought out a motor cycle that was a type between a cycle and a vehicle. It had two front steering wheels and one front driver. The same type of vehicle has been adopted for light work, such as parcel delivery.

Joseph Guedon

Guedon made his appearance at Bordeaux, in October, 1897, with a four-wheeled wagonette, which he made under the name of the Decauville. His special construction was claimed to very largely eliminate the vibration of the vehicle, and his success can be fairly judged from the results in the past few years. The Decauville cars have been developed and refined to such a point as to be among the best of the French makes, and now have an international reputation.

RENE DE KNYFF

De Knyff became an enthusiastic automobilist, and with other gentlemen, sportsmen of the nobility, became a great amateur. He was and is still known as the King of Chauffeurs, having won several of the most important races, driving the Panhard cars to victory.

ADOLF CLEMENT

Born in 1855.

Entirely a self-made man, Clement had experience as a locksmith and served an apprenticeship as a tinsmith. He started and built up a bicycle manufacturing establishment which, in 1894, was considered one of the finest in France. In time this developed into the finest cycle manufactory in that country. It is situated in Levallois, near Paris. In 1899, Clement contracted with Panhard & Levassor to manufacture under their patents, and in 1900 he made a most successful light vehicle of four horse-power. Since then he has developed his automobile factory, and in the past few years has produced competitors for honors in the first class, which are known at home and abroad as the Bayard or Clement-Bayard cars.

A. DARRACQ

About fifty years of age, Darracq has had an energetic and successful career. He is now president of the Society of Engineers, Paris, and a member of the Legion of Honor. He is best known as an inventor in connection with the automobile industry. Among his inventions are a shaft drive and a beveled gear drive which are now universally used. He originated the idea of placing the operating lever on the steering post and made the first moderate priced automobile in France. He is now the engineer and manager of one of the biggest factories in the world.

JAMES GORDON BENNETT

So interesting was the sporting side of the automobile movement that it early attracted the attention of James Gordon Bennett. The great runs, or tours, or races commenced in 1891, and continued annually from 1894 on, resulted in the offering of the Bennett trophy for international competition under conditions which may have been suggested by the America yacht cup races. In January, 1900, this was announced in Paris, and the custody of the trophy initially given to the Automobile Club of France as the first and foremost champions of automobiling. Elaborate and excellent rules govern the annual competition for the trophy, and the races are held in the country whose representative has won in the previous year. In this way the first race was in France, as well as the second, and the 1903 race in Ireland, while that of 1904 was held in Germany, but was won by a Frenchman, so that the 1905 race will again be held in the land of the original custodians of the trophy.

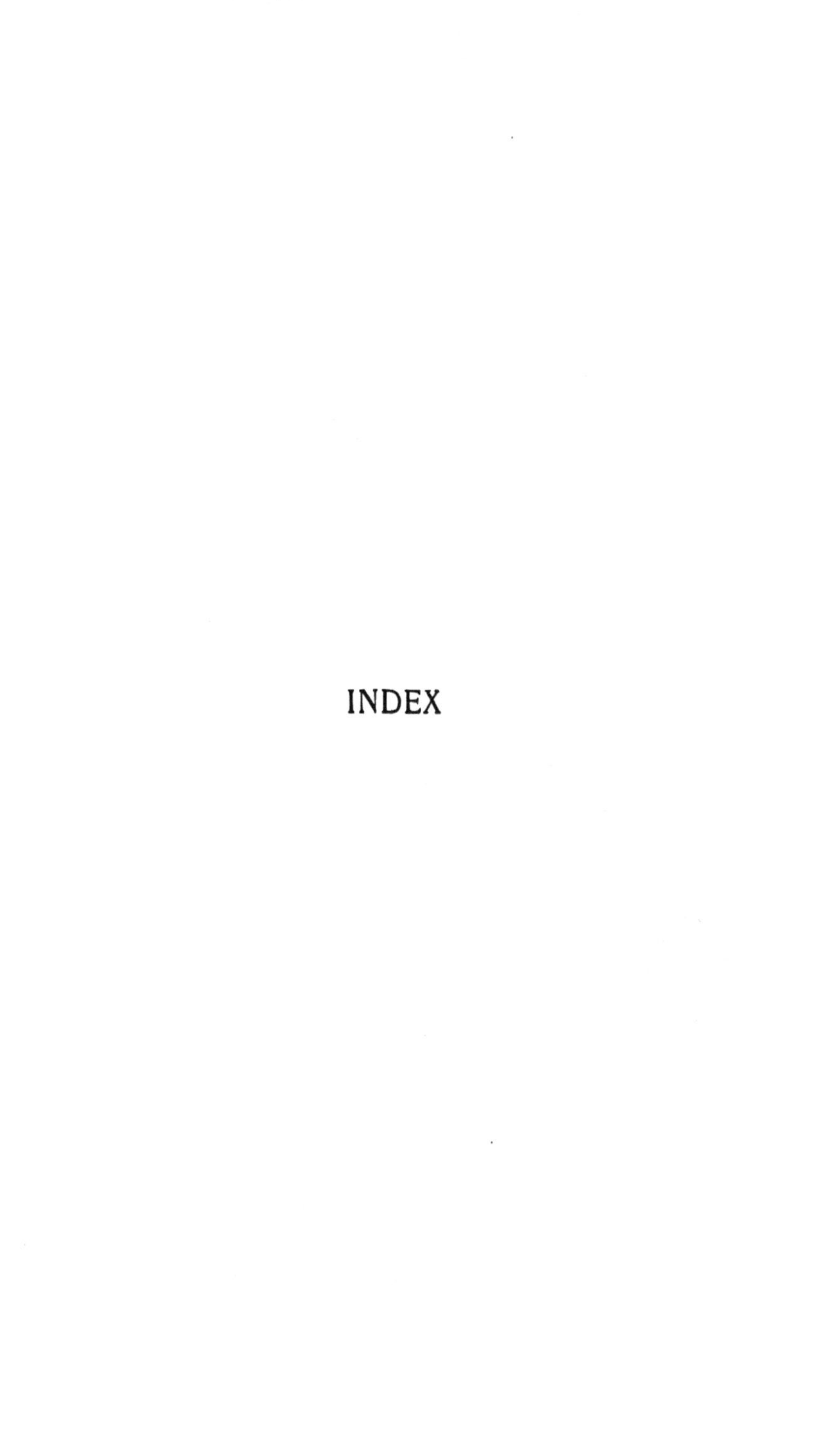

INDEX

INDEX

INDEX

Zeitfracht Medien GmbH
Ferdinand-Jühlke-Straße 7
99095 Erfurt, Deutschland
produktsicherheit@kolibri360.de